D0535867

INSIDE FORENSIC SCIENCE

Forensic Pharmacology

INSIDE FORENSIC SCIENCE

Forensic Anthropology

Forensic DNA Analysis

Forensic Medicine

Forensic Pharmacology

Legal Aspects of Forensics

The Forensic Aspects of Poisons

INSIDE FORENSIC SCIENCE

Forensic Pharmacology

Beth E. Zedeck, MSW, RN, MSN
and Morris S. Zedeck, Ph.D.

SERIES EDITOR | Lawrence Kobilinsky, Ph.D.

CHELSEA HOUSE PUBLISHERS
An imprint of Infobase Publishing

The authors are proud to have worked as a father and daughter team on this project and wish to thank Dr. Zedeck's wife, Ellen Lieberman, Esq., for her assistance and thoughtful suggestions during the preparation of this book.

Forensic Pharmacology

Copyright © 2007 by Infobase Publishing

Chelsea House
An imprint of Infobase Publishing
132 West 31st Street
New York NY 10001

Library of Congress Cataloging-in-Publication Data
Zedeck, Beth E.
    Forensic pharmacology / Beth E. Zedeck and Morris S. Zedeck.
        p. cm. — (Inside forensic science)
    Includes bibliographical references and index.
    ISBN 0-7910-8920-7 (hardcover)
    1. Forensic pharmacology. I. Zedeck, Morris S. II. Title.
RA1160.Z43 2006
614'.1—dc22
                                                        2006020624

Chelsea House books are available at special discounts when purchased in bulk quantities for businesses, associations, institutions, or sales promotions. Please call our Special Sales Department in New York at (212) 967-8800 or (800) 322-8755.

You can find Chelsea House on the World Wide Web at http://www.chelseahouse.com

Cover design by Ben Peterson
Text design by Annie O'Donnell

Printed in the United States of America

BANG FOF 10 9 8 7 6 5 4 3 2 1

This book is printed on acid-free paper.

All links and Web addresses were checked and verified to be correct at the time of publication. Because of the dynamic nature of the Web, some addresses and links may have changed since publication and may no longer be valid.

Table of Contents

Introduction: The Role of the Forensic Pharmacologist

Today, through television, most Americans have been exposed to the application of **forensic science** to the justice system. Programs such as *Law and Order, CSI, Crossing Jordan, Cold Case Files, Forensic Files*, and *American Justice* feature police activities, forensic laboratory technology, and courtroom procedures. These programs have made the public aware of the important role that forensic science plays in the criminal justice system, and enrollment in criminal justice and forensic science courses in college and high school has increased markedly within the last 10 years.

As a result of increased exposure to the work of forensic scientists, juror selection has become more difficult, since jurors now expect prosecutors to provide evidence as easily and as rapidly as seen on television. In selecting a jury panel, lawyers are aware that these television programs may influence jurors (called the "CSI effect") and the absence of expected evidence might work against the prosecutor in criminal cases.

Public attention is also drawn to the death of celebrities resulting from **drug** overdose. For example, Janis Joplin, the blues singer, overdosed on heroin, actor River Phoenix and comedian

John Belushi both overdosed on speedballs, a mixture of heroin and cocaine, and college basketball star Len Bias and Cleveland Browns football player Don Rogers both overdosed on cocaine.

Have you ever wondered how scientists determine whether a drug was involved in a particular case, and whether the amount of drug is considered an overdose and thus was the cause of death? Today many job applicants must submit a pre-employment urine sample to test for the presence of drugs, and random urine tests are performed on many individuals in high-stress jobs, including police officers, firefighters, pilots, and truck drivers. Have you wondered how such tests are performed to determine presence and quantity of drug? Are you curious to learn why alcohol is detected in breath samples? All of these issues fall under the broad heading of forensic science.

WHAT IS FORENSIC SCIENCE?

Forensic science can be defined as the application of science to legal issues. The role of science in resolving legal matters has increased substantially over the last 50 years. During this period, major advances in technology and information gathering have been made in the areas of medicine, molecular biology, analytical chemistry, computer science, and microscopy. Because the information and methodologies in these areas of science are so vast and complex, the law has become dependent on testimony by scientists to help unravel complex legal cases involving biological and physical evidence. Areas of science that may require explanation by experts include **pharmacology**, the study of all effects of chemicals on living organisms, and **toxicology**, the study of the toxic or adverse effects of chemicals, which are both the subjects of this book. There are other areas that require expert testimony, including DNA analysis, forensic medicine (anatomy and **pathology**), forensic odontology

FIGURE 1.1 Pharmacologist Dr. Donald H. Catlin sits in front of an LC/MS/MS system, an instrument used for detecting drugs from urine samples, at the UCLA Olympic Analytical Laboratory. Catlin is noted for developing a breakthrough test that detects the illegal steroid, tetrahydrogestrinone (THG), taken by athletes to enhance performance.

(dentistry), criminalistics (analysis of physical evidence such as hair, fibers, blood, paint, glass, soil, arson-related chemicals, and solid drug samples), questioned document examination (analysis of inks and papers), forensic engineering (accident reconstruction, environmental and construction analysis), firearm and toolmark analysis, forensic anthropology (analysis of bodily remains), forensic entomology (analysis of insects on deceased individuals to determine time of death), forensic psychology, voice pattern analysis, fingerprint analysis, and forensic nursing (effects of sexual assault and trauma).

A **pharmacologist** is a scientist who, in addition to being trained in the principles of pharmacology, studies other disciplines, including physiology, biochemistry, chemistry, molecular biology, statistics, and pathology, and usually possesses a Ph.D. degree (Figure 1.1). Pharmacology programs require a minimum of four years of graduate study, including a doctoral dissertation of original research. Chemicals studied by a pharmacologist may be natural (from plants or animals) or synthetic, and may include medicinals, drugs of abuse, poisons, carcinogens, and industrial chemicals. The pharmacologist must understand how chemicals interact with the most basic cell components such as receptors and DNA, and must explain how such interactions produce the observed results. The pharmacologist studies chemicals for their beneficial or therapeutic effects as well as their adverse or toxic effects. A **toxicologist**, usually someone with a Ph.D. degree, uses the same principles of science as the pharmacologist but generally studies only toxic or adverse effects of chemicals. Others working in a pharmacology or toxicology laboratory often have master or bachelor of science degrees in various specialties and are trained in experimentation and analytical procedures.

One of the basic principles of toxicology is that chemicals that are safe in appropriate doses can become toxic in higher doses. Even too much water can become toxic. Pharmacologists and toxicologists rely on dose-response tests, in which the effects of drugs are measured at different doses to see the relationship between dose and effect and, as the dosage increases, how the effect can quickly go from no effect to a desired effect to a toxic effect level. When studying chemicals, it is important to keep in mind a phrase of the famous fifteenth-century alchemist and physician Paracelsus (born Theophrastus Philippus Aureolus Bombastus von Hohenheim): "Is there anything that is not a poison? Everything is poison, and nothing is without poison. The dose alone makes a thing poisonous."[1]

This book will focus on forensic pharmacology and drugs of abuse. Drugs of abuse, such as cocaine, heroin, marijuana, PCP, benzodiazepines, and methamphetamine, are often involved in criminal and civil matters concerning personal injury, motor vehicle accidents, drug overdose, and murder, and thus, are discussed to illustrate forensic pharmacology issues and investigations.

What is forensic pharmacology and how does it differ from forensic toxicology? Both disciplines attempt to answer the question of whether a chemical was causally related to an individual's behavior, illness, injury, or death. The effect of the chemical might occur soon after exposure (an acute effect) or a long time after exposure (a chronic effect). To establish what caused the effect, scientists examine bodily tissues and fluids for the presence of drugs and, using different analytical techniques, identify chemicals and determine their concentration. Besides the obvious fluids of blood and urine, analysis can be performed on nails, hair, bone, semen, amniotic fluid, stomach contents, breast milk, **vitreous humor** (the fluid inside the eyeball), sweat, and saliva. What fluids and tissues are analyzed depends on the type of case and whether the subject is alive or deceased. Understanding of the chemical's **pharmacodynamics**, the mechanisms that bring about physiological and pathological changes, and **pharmacokinetics,** how the chemical is absorbed, distributed, metabolized, and excreted, are important in establishing a causal relationship. For example, once the concentration of a chemical and its **metabolites** in blood and/or urine are determined, it might be possible to determine when the drug was administered or taken. Interpretation of the findings, in relation to other facts and evidence in the case, may help solve a crime. On occasion, any items at a crime scene that may be drug related, such as syringes or vials containing a solution, are also brought to the forensic laboratory for analysis.

FORENSIC SCIENTISTS AT WORK

Most often, pharmacologists conduct research programs while employed in private, government, and commercial research laboratories, hospitals, and academic institutions. A pharmacologist may be contacted by an attorney and asked to consult or testify as an **expert witness** in legal matters that may be either criminal or civil and for the **plaintiff** or **defendant** (Figure 1.2). Attorneys learn of expert witnesses from advertisements in legal newspapers and journals, and by calling referral agencies that maintain lists of specialists in areas of medicine, science, engineering, finance, construction, aviation, and so on.

Interpretation of chemical data obtained from analysis of bodily fluids and tissues by a pharmacologist may help attorneys

FIGURE 1.2   In the photograph above, Dr. Jo Ellen Dyer, a pharmacist and toxicologist who specializes in GHB and sexual assault, serves as an expert witness at the rape trial of Max Factor heir, Andrew Luster. In 2003, Luster was convicted of raping a series of women after he used GHB, a "date rape" drug, to seduce his victims.

determine the role of a drug in an individual's behavior or death. If, for example, analysis shows a deceased person was under the influence of drugs, such data along with other facts in the case may help determine if death was due to an accidental overdose, suicide, or homicide by poisoning. In murder cases, it is important to know whether the deceased was under the influence of drugs. The prosecutor is interested, since it may explain the behavior of the deceased just before death, and the results may suggest to the defense attorney that a defendant charged with murder could have acted in self-defense. In civil lawsuits resulting from motor vehicle accidents or injuries from falls, whether those involved were under the influence of drugs may be an important factor.

The forensic pharmacologist will first review analytic reports to determine whether the data support the attorney's position. The review will focus on the positive aspects as well as on any areas that may be problematic in the case. The findings are presented to the attorney along with information that will help the attorney understand the science. If the pharmacologist's opinion is supportive, the attorney may request a written report. In many civil lawsuits, the use of experts results in settlements rather than trials. If the case goes to trial and the pharmacologist is expected to testify, the pharmacologist will assist the attorney in preparing a proper examination so that the testimony presented to the jury will be a clear and understandable explanation of the findings. Finally, the pharmacologist may assist the attorney in preparing a cross-examination of the opposing side's expert witness.

Forensic toxicologists are generally employed by federal, state, and local government crime laboratories, which may be affiliated with the medical examiner's office from which they receive fluids and tissues for analysis. They often work on criminal cases and usually testify for the office of the district attorney, the prosecutor. Forensic toxicologists may also be involved in drug testing in

History of Pharmacology and Toxicology

The science of pharmacology began with Rudolf Buchheim, a German pharmacologist who lived between 1820 and 1879. At the University of Dorpat in Russia (now Tartu in Estonia), he built a laboratory and began a systematic study of drug action. A pupil of Buchheim, Oswald Schmiedeberg succeeded Buchheim at Dorpat in 1866. Later, Schmiedeberg moved to Strasbourg, France, and developed a very successful program in pharmacology. Students came from all over the world. One of the students was John Jacob Abel, who then returned to the United States and became chairman of the first pharmacology department in a medical school, at the University of Michigan, in 1891. Abel is considered the father of American pharmacology, and played a major role in the organization of the American Society for Pharmacology and Experimental Therapeutics (ASPET). Today, pharmacology is part of the educational programs at medical, nursing, pharmacy, and other health professional schools.

Some of the earliest forensic toxicologists were Alexander Gettler, Raymond Abernethy, and Rutherford Gradwohl. In their time, analytical instruments and procedures were in their infancy, but they developed many of the techniques used today in chemical analysis. They were founders of the American Academy of Forensic Sciences (AAFS) in 1948. Today, the AAFS is divided among 10 sections: criminalistics, engineering sciences, general, jurisprudence, odontology, pathology/biology, physical anthropology, psychiatry and behavioral sciences, questioned documents, and toxicology.

the workplace or in sports. The pharmacologist may be involved in a broader scope of forensic issues than the toxicologist, with such diverse cases as adverse drug reactions to medicines, overdose of medicines, drug interactions, personal injury following exposure to medicines, effects from drugs of abuse or industrial chemicals, and induction of cancer by chemicals.

REAL-LIFE CASES

One of the authors has testified in court as an expert witness on many drug-related issues, including unexpected reactions to a medicine, whether a person accused of assault or murder of an attacker who had high blood levels of drugs of abuse could reasonably claim self-defense, whether exposure to medicinal chemicals, industrial chemicals, mercury-containing herbal preparations, carbon monoxide, or lead paint could have caused certain injuries or illnesses, whether drugs could have affected the behavior of people involved in motor vehicle accidents or accused of murder, and whether the presence of drugs of abuse in urine can be explained by reasons other than intentional drug abuse. Examples from these actual forensic pharmacology cases will be presented in the individual drug chapters.

As an example of an actual criminal case, two defendants were accused of raping a woman they had invited to their apartment. They claimed that the victim drank herself into a stupor within about 30 minutes after arrival, that she imagined the rape occurred, and that she left on her own about four hours later. The victim testified that she had two beers and one scotch within a 2.5-hour period. At some point she excused herself to make a phone call. Shortly after she returned and finished her drink, she felt dizzy and lost consciousness. She awoke briefly to find herself being raped but was weak, in a dreamlike state, and could not speak or move. She was able to leave about two hours later with the assistance of family members. The author's testimony before the jury explained that the amount of alcohol consumed by the victim was insufficient to induce unconsciousness and that if enough alcohol had been consumed to reach a level of unconsciousness, as the defendants claimed, given the rate of alcohol metabolism, it is highly unlikely a person would appear relatively normal several hours later. The author's opinion was that when the victim left the room to make the phone call, it is likely that drugs were added to her drink. This testimony, along with other evidence, helped the jury find the two defendants guilty, and they were sentenced to up to 25 years in prison.

As an example of an actual civil case not involving drugs of abuse, an infant developed seizures after being hospitalized for fever. Analysis of the infant's bodily fluids revealed the presence of high levels of theophylline, a drug used to treat asthma that in high doses can cause seizures. The plaintiff alleged that an error occurred in the hospital and that the infant was given theophylline instead of an antibiotic. At trial, the hospital countered that the theophylline in the infant came from the mother's breast milk, since the mother was taking theophylline for asthma and was breast-feeding her child. Theophylline pharmacokinetic data were presented to the jury indicating that the amount of theophylline excreted via breast milk could never account for the levels found in the infant. An error in drug administration probably occurred. The parties settled the lawsuit.

This book will outline what forensic pharmacology is and how it is used in similar cases in the real world. Chapter 2 will describe principles used by forensic pharmacologists to establish causation, namely pharmacokinetics and pharmacodynamics. Chapter 3 will describe the tools used by forensic scientists to identify and quantify chemicals in bodily fluids and tissues. Chapter 4 will describe current trends in drug abuse, focusing on drug abuse by adolescents. Chapters 5 to 12 will describe the pharmacology of eight major categories of drugs of abuse as well as interesting forensic issues for many of the drugs. Chapter 13 will discuss the future of forensic pharmacology, and Chapter 14 will test the reader's knowledge by presenting several cases for the reader to solve. There are hundreds of street names for many of the drugs of abuse. We have selected a few names from select resources for each drug, and the bibliography and further reading list should be consulted for additional references.

2

Pharmacokinetics and Pharmacodynamics

The first aspect of pharmacokinetics involves the entry of a drug into the body. Chemicals, in the form of foods, medicines, drugs of abuse, or industrial chemicals, can enter the human body via several routes, including ingestion, inhalation, injection, skin application, and suppository. Except for cases of injection directly into the bloodstream, the chemical must pass through complex living cell membranes before it can enter the bloodstream.

For example, chemicals that enter the digestive tract must be absorbed by the cells lining the small intestine and then be transferred through the cells, where the chemical can then be absorbed by the capillary cells into the bloodstream. Chemicals that are inhaled must pass through the **alveoli**, the cells of the lungs, to get to the capillaries and enter the bloodstream.

As chemicals pass into and out of cells, they must cross the cell membrane that keeps all of the cell contents securely inside, but which allows some materials to pass (Figure 2.1). Chemicals can move through the cell membrane through one of several mechanisms.

One of the mechanisms for moving chemicals through the cell membrane is passive **diffusion**, which is based on the difference

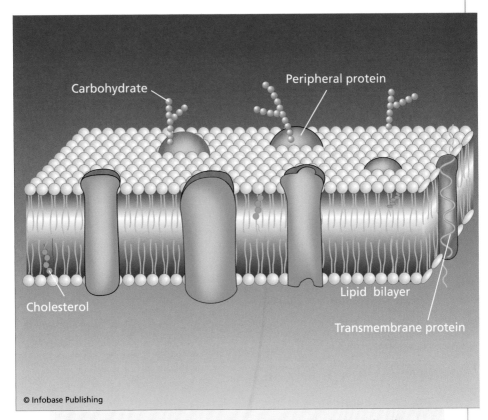

FIGURE 2.1 The cell membrane consists mainly of lipids (fats), proteins, and carbohydrates in the form of a lipid bilayer. The two lipid layers face each other inside the membrane, and the water-soluble phosphate groups of the membrane face the watery contents inside the cell (the cytoplasm) and outside the cell (the interstitial fluid).

in concentration of the chemical outside of the cell compared to inside the cell. The greater the difference, the greater the movement of the chemical to the inside of the cell. Since the membrane is highly lipid in nature, **lipophilic** (lipid-loving) chemicals will diffuse more easily across the membrane. Ionized molecules that are more water soluble do not diffuse across membranes as readily as lipophilic molecules and are influenced by the **pH** of the fluid surrounding the cell. Water-soluble chemicals can also be transported using carrier proteins, and this process is called facilitated diffusion.

Inorganic ions, such as sodium and potassium, move through the cell membrane by active transport. Unlike diffusion, energy is required for active transport as the chemical is moving from a lower concentration to a higher one. One example is the sodium-potassium ATPase pump, which transports sodium $[Na^+]$ ions out of the cell and potassium $[K^+]$ into the cell.

Chemicals may cross the cell membrane via membrane pores. This diffusion depends on the size of the pore and the size and weight of the chemical. The chemical flows through the membrane along with water. Finally, the membrane can actually engulf the chemical, form a small pouch called a vesicle, and transport it across the membrane to the inside of the cell. This process is called pinocytosis.

DISTRIBUTION OF CHEMICALS

Once the chemical is in the bloodstream, it can be distributed to various organs. Initially its concentration in blood is greater than in tissues. Because of the difference in concentration, the chemical will leave the blood and enter the surrounding cells.

Sometimes other factors affect the movement of the chemical. For example, not all chemicals easily enter the brain. The capillary cells in the brain have tight junctions restricting the flow of materials between cells. One type of cell forms a tight covering on the capillary and prevents or slows down large molecules from passing through the cells. This structure is known as the **blood-brain barrier**. All of the drugs discussed in this book—drugs of abuse—affect the **central nervous system (CNS)**, which consists of the brain and spinal cord. Thus, the drug must pass through the blood-brain barrier.

The availability of a chemical to the cells is affected by where it is stored. First, lipophilic chemicals tend to get absorbed by and retained in fat cells, from which they are released slowly back into the bloodstream. Second, some chemicals are strongly bound to plasma proteins and are released to the cells more slowly over time. For example, acetaminophen (Tylenol®) does not bind strongly to plasma proteins, while diazepam (Valium®) does. Thus, diazepam will persist in the body for longer periods of time than will acetaminophen. Finally, some elements, such as fluorine, lead, and strontium, are bound up in bone for long periods of time. As bone slowly renews itself or is broken down under special circumstances such as pregnancy, the chemicals are released and can affect the mother and fetus.

METABOLISM OF CHEMICALS

Many **xenobiotics**, or chemicals that are foreign to the body, undergo metabolism. This type of metabolism is different from the metabolism of food nutrients necessary for production of energy to drive bodily functions. The purpose of xenobiotic metabolism is to convert active chemicals into inactive forms or convert inactive chemicals into active ones, and to transform chemicals into more water-soluble forms so that they can be more easily excreted via the urine and bile. To understand drug action, it is important to know whether the original chemical or the product of its metabolism (its metabolites), or both, is responsible for the pharmacological effects.

While many tissues can metabolize foreign chemicals, metabolism of xenobiotics primarily occurs in the liver. It is important to note that everything that is ingested and passes into the intestine first passes through the liver before entering the general circulation. Thus, you can think of the liver as the filter for the entire body.

Metabolism of xenobiotics proceeds via a two-stage process. Phase I consists of oxidation, reduction, or hydrolysis to form polar groups such as hydroxyl (OH) or carboxyl (COOH). Phase II consists of conjugation, whereby enzymes add to the polar groups glucuronic acid, sulfate, acetate, or glutathione, making the chemical more water soluble. Sometimes, the new metabolite is as active or more active than the parent chemical. Such an example is morphine-6-**glucuronide**, which is as active as morphine.

Phase I enzymes, located in the **endoplasmic reticulum**, include cytochrome P450-dependent monooxygenases. There are many genes for the different cytochrome P450 (CYP) enzymes, each acting on different sets of chemicals. Another Phase I enzyme, monoamine oxidase (MAO), can be found in mitochondria. The enzymes involved in Phase II metabolism are found mainly in the cytoplasm. Also in the cytoplasm is the enzyme alcohol dehydrogenase that metabolizes ethanol (drinking alcohol) to acetaldehyde which is then metabolized to acetic acid. Interestingly, exposure to the xenobiotic chemical sometimes increases the amount of the enzyme used for its own metabolism.

Since one particular enzyme system can metabolize many different chemicals, there is great potential for drug interaction. If one drug can increase the level of a specific enzyme, a second drug metabolized by that enzyme would also be more quickly metabolized. This may result in enhanced activity or a lowering of the drug's blood level and decreased effectiveness of one or both drugs. Also, if two drugs compete for an enzyme's activity, each drug might be metabolized more slowly, thereby prolonging their effects. Such information may be important in legal cases involving toxic effects of chemicals as a result of drug interaction.

Some people are rapid metabolizers of drugs and some are slow metabolizers. Factors that can affect the response to drugs include age, gender, and genetics. Very young children and older people metabolize drugs more slowly. There are some differences seen between men and women, as well as between races, in the metabolism of certain drugs. A new field of pharmacogenomics studies the role of genes in drug action and will someday allow for study of an individual's genes to determine in advance the response to drug therapy.

It is important to know how much of the chemical is destroyed as it passes through the liver to enter the general circulation. If, for example, someone ingests 100 milligrams of drug A and only 50 milligrams exits from the liver, then 50% of the drug was lost. This is known as the first-pass effect. Using this example, if 200 milligrams is required for a therapeutic effect, then a pharmaceutical manufacturer must incorporate 400 milligrams into each tablet. First-pass metabolism influences the effects of several drugs of abuse.

EXCRETION OF CHEMICALS

Chemicals and/or their metabolites are eventually eliminated. The three organs predominantly involved in elimination are the liver, the lungs, and the kidneys. Other routes of excretion include bile, feces, sweat, saliva, breast milk, nails, and hair.

As blood passes through the lungs for exchange of carbon dioxide and oxygen, volatile chemicals such as alcohol exit from the blood and are exhaled. Drugs that are eliminated via the bile are excreted into the small intestine and then eliminated via the feces, though some drugs are partly reabsorbed. This pattern of circulation, called enterohepatic circulation, from bile to intestine and back to liver, continues until the drug is completely eliminated. Blood is filtered as it passes through the kidney, and chemicals can leave the blood to become part of the urine forming in the renal tubules.

As a result of metabolism and excretion, drugs leave the body at certain rates. The rate of elimination may vary widely with different drugs, which explains why some medications must be taken four times daily, while others are taken only once a day. The **half-life** of a drug is the time in which the concentration of drug, generally in blood or **plasma**, decreases by 50%. Thus, if drug X has a half-life of three hours, and after absorption of drug X the blood concentration is 100 units, then three hours later the concentration would be 50 units, and three hours after that the blood concentration would be 25 units. After five half-lives, the concentration of drug X would be approximately 3% of the initial value. To maintain therapeutic levels of drug X, you might require taking a dose every three hours. Knowledge of excretion patterns of a chemical and of its metabolites is important for determining treatment schedules as well as for determining, in criminal or civil matters, when a drug had been taken or administered.

PHARMACODYNAMICS

Pharmacodynamics is the study of the mechanisms of drug action. How does a chemical cure disease, stimulate or inhibit the nervous system, change behavior, influence our digestive system, or induce a toxic reaction? The body itself is made up of chemicals, and when drugs (chemicals) are taken, the drugs interact with the body's chemicals and these interactions result in biochemical and physiological effects. While there are many different mechanisms of drug action that account for the different effects of diverse drugs, in this book we will restrict our discussion to those reactions that explain the effects of drugs of abuse. Drugs of abuse bring about their effects by interacting with cell receptors or by influencing the levels of various neurotransmitters, outlined below.

Cell Receptors

A receptor is a macromolecule on or in a cell with which a drug can interact and begin a sequence of events eventually leading to an effect. There are many receptors, some specific to a tissue or organ and others that are found more generally. Receptors include enzymes, regulatory proteins, and DNA-binding proteins. Often, the first reaction between chemical and receptor brings about a chain of reactions before the final effect is

The Science of Anatomy

The study of anatomy was originally restricted to animals. In the fourteenth century, an Italian named Mondino de' Liucci performed human dissection and published his findings. Leonardo da Vinci, born in the fifteenth century, was recognized as a painter, a scientist, and an engineer. His most famous paintings are the *Mona Lisa* and *The Last Supper*. Da Vinci was also interested in human anatomy and published the first textbook on human anatomy. Andreas Vesalius, a physician, was influenced by da Vinci's work. Vesalius published a seven-volume collection detailing the human body entitled *De Humani Corporis Fabrica*. In the eighteenth century, medical students were allowed to perform human dissection. In England, in 1858, Dr. Henry Gray published his first book, entitled *Anatomy, Descriptive and Surgical*. Today, many people know this book as *Gray's Anatomy*. In 1989, Frank H. Netter, a physician and medical illustrator, published his extremely detailed anatomical drawings in full color, termed *Atlas of Human Anatomy*.

produced. Drugs that bring about effects are called agonists. Chemicals that can block effects are termed antagonists.

Neuronal Signaling

At the end of each neuron are stores of chemicals called neurotransmitters that can be released to stimulate adjacent neurons (Figure 2.2). There are many different neurotransmitters, dependent on location and specific function in the nervous system. Generally, once a neuron is stimulated, the stimulus travels along the neuronal axon until it reaches the end of the neuron from which a neurotransmitter is released. The neurotrans-

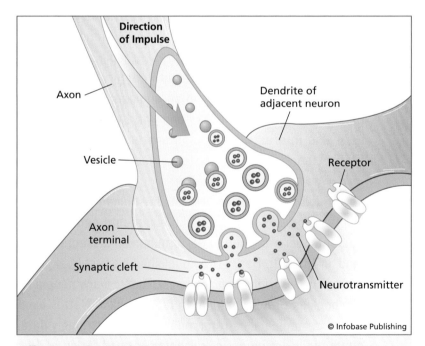

© Infobase Publishing

Figure 2.2   In this illustration of neuronal signaling, an electrical impulse causes the release of neurotransmitters from vesicles in the axon terminal of a neuron. The neurotransmitters cross the synapse (also known as the synaptic cleft) and bind to receptors on a receiving neuron.

mitter enters a space between the neuron it was released from and adjacent neurons. This space is called a synapse. The neurotransmitter diffuses across the synapse and excites a receptor on an adjacent neuron. Any chemical that has not attached itself to the surrounding neurons can either be destroyed by enzymes or be taken back up into the original neuron. Drugs can affect the function of the nervous system in several ways. They can stimulate or inhibit release of neurotransmitter, block its effects or affect its metabolism, prevent reuptake of the neurotransmitter, or mimic the effects of a neurotransmitter. Some examples of neurotransmitters in the CNS affected by drugs of abuse include gamma-aminobutyric acid (GABA), norepinephrine and dopamine, serotonin, endorphins, dynorphins, and enkephalins, and glutamate.

- Gamma-aminobutyric acid (GABA), is present in many areas of the brain, and is inhibitory. GABA can influence sensation of pain and affects memory, mood, and coordination. GHB and benzodiazepines increase GABA activity.

- Norepinephrine and dopamine are stimulants and increase mental alertness. Amphetamines activate norepinephrine receptors and also release norepinephrine and dopamine from storage; cocaine blocks the reuptake of dopamine.

- Serotonin (5HT) affects sleep, temperature, sexual behavior, sensory perception, appetite, and mood. There are many serotonin receptors, and activation of each brings about different effects. LSD and psilocybin activate serotonin receptors.

- Endorphins, dynorphins, and enkephalins are natural peptide neurotransmitters that activate the opioid receptors and affect sensation of pain, and induce **euphoria**, a feeling of well-being or elation.

- Glutamate activates the N-methyl-D-aspartate (NMDA) receptor. Glutamate is involved in perception of pain, sensory input, and memory. PCP and dextromethorphan block this receptor.

- The enzyme MAO metabolizes some of the neurotransmitters affected by some drugs of abuse, namely epinephrine, norepinephrine, dopamine, and serotonin. Dangerously high levels can result if an inhibitor of this enzyme, or **monoamine oxidase inhibitor (MAOI)**, is used along with the drug of abuse.

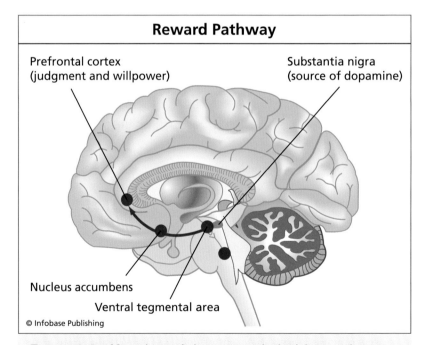

Reward Pathway

Prefrontal cortex (judgment and willpower)

Substantia nigra (source of dopamine)

Nucleus accumbens

Ventral tegmental area

© Infobase Publishing

FIGURE 2.3 Many drugs of abuse act on the brain's reward center, which is illustrated above. The drugs cause neurons in the ventral tegmental area to release dopamine. The dopamine, in turn, initiates a chain of events that results in feelings of enjoyment and pleasure.

Many of the effects of drugs of abuse have been localized to what is termed the brain's reward center (Figure 2.3). The drugs increase the concentration of the neurotransmitter dopamine in the mesolimbic dopaminergic system. This system includes those areas of the brain designated as the ventral tegmental area (VTA), which transmits signals to the nucleus accumbens, prefrontal cortex, and other areas of the brain. All together these are considered the reward and drug seeking areas of the brain.

SUMMARY

The cell membrane is a complex structure of lipid, protein, and carbohydrate and regulates chemical passage via several mechanisms. Chemicals can interact with cell membranes or be absorbed into a cell to exert their pharmacologic effects. Chemicals reach their target via the bloodstream, and intracellular concentration is dependent on the extent of plasma protein binding. Most chemicals undergo some form of metabolism to be either activated or inactivated, or, in some cases, both. Lipid-soluble molecules tend to be deposited in fat cells and are released slowly over time. Eventually, chemicals are eliminated, most often via urine and feces. Drugs of abuse bring about their effects by interacting with cell receptors or by influencing the levels of various neurotransmitters.

Drug Analysis

One role of the forensic scientist is to help determine whether drugs caused the behavior, illness, injury, or death of an individual. To do this with some scientific basis, the scientist must determine whether a drug or active metabolite is present in bodily fluids and tissues, and, if so, its concentration. It is the concentration of drug in blood and inside the cell that relates to pharmacologic effects (dose-response relationship), and the concentration inside the cell closely approximates the concentration in blood. Thus, analysis of a sample of blood, plasma, or **serum** (the liquid part of the blood remaining after clotting) is best for establishing a direct connection. While a drug or metabolite may be detected in urine, such evidence is indicative of prior exposure to the drug, but the concentration may not be related to the observed effects.

When dealing with deceased individuals, the forensic pathologist (usually the medical examiner) will provide samples of blood taken from both the heart and the leg's femoral vein. The results will be compared to avoid reaching an incorrect conclusion of drug concentration for those drugs that exhibit **postmortem redistribution**, which is when substances that were concentrated in heart and adjacent organs leak back out into the blood and produce abnormally high values. The forensic scientist may also receive samples of urine, bile, vitreous humor, and tissue from various organs such as liver, kidney, lung, heart, and brain, as well as stomach contents, to determine if large amounts of a drug had been ingested. Analysis of these tissues could give a clearer picture of whether any drugs present had a direct connection to the manner of death, whether it be natural, suicide, homicide, or accidental.

Analysis of tissues such as nails, hair, and bone, where chemicals are deposited but not readily released (Figure 3.1), is useful to determine whether an individual had ever been exposed to a particular chemical, but is of less value in determining recent exposure and causation.

ANALYTICAL TESTS

The forensic scientist has multiple analytic techniques available. Some are screening tests that may not absolutely identify the chemical in question but narrow the number of possibilities. Subsequently, the analyst will perform confirmatory tests in which the chemical is positively identified. It is important to remember that even though the analysis may reveal the presence of a drug, there may be a legitimate reason for such a finding. We will discuss such examples in individual chapters.

There are two types of analysis: qualitative and quantitative. Qualitative analysis determines which chemical is present, while quantitative analysis determines the concentration of a chemical. Concentration means an amount of chemical per unit of sample, for example, 100 micrograms (µg) of morphine per liter (L) of blood (100 µg/L); or the amount of pure chemical per weight of material, such as 1 gram of heroin per 10 grams of white powder.

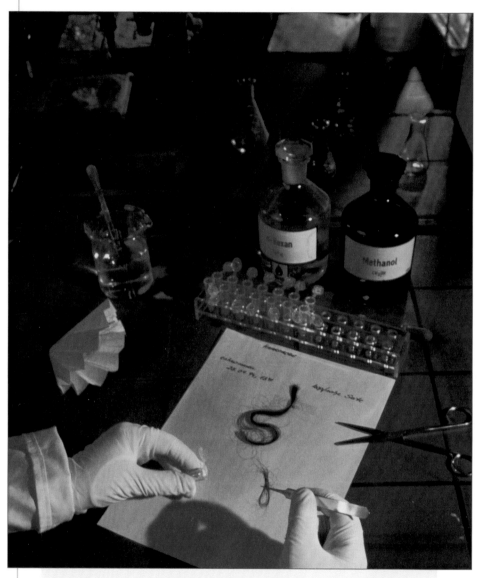

FIGURE 3.1 A hair sample from a suspected drug user is prepared for forensic analysis. As hair grows, it incorporates small amounts of chemicals that are produced when drugs are broken down in the body. To identify these drugs, the hair is first cut into pieces and soaked in a liquid solvent. The solvent removes the traces of drug metabolites from the hair so that they can be identified by chromatography and mass spectrometry.

Important considerations in any type of test include **specificity** and **sensitivity**. Specificity refers to the ability of a test to detect only the compound in question and not mistakenly identify other compounds in the sample (which is known as a false positive). Sensitivity refers to how reliably a test will detect the compound in question when it is present in a sample. A less sensitive test will sometimes fail to detect the presence of a compound.

When samples are received in the laboratory, they are often first treated by various extraction procedures to separate any chemicals from the original fluid or tissue. The extract is then analyzed by screening or confirmatory procedures.

On occasion it becomes necessary to dig up, or **exhume**, a body and to test for the presence of drugs. Such analysis presents special problems for the forensic scientist. First, the blood has been displaced with embalming fluid, and blood levels are not obtainable; second, the drug may have decomposed in air or moisture or been chemically altered by the embalming fluid or by bacteria growing on decomposing tissue; and third, the tissues may have completely decomposed. Although teeth, bone, or nails may be present, death may have occurred too soon for the drug to have accumulated in these tissues. Interpretation of data and any conclusions drawn using exhumed samples must be done with caution.

A notable case involving exhumation is that of Dr. X. In 1976, Dr. Mario E. Jascalevich, known as Dr. X before his true identity was revealed, was accused of murdering five patients 10 years earlier at Riverdell Hospital in Oradell, New Jersey, by administering curare, a muscle relaxant. The five bodies were exhumed, and toxicology results were presented at trial that lasted 34 weeks. A key argument between the prosecution and defense expert witnesses was whether curare was in fact detected in the bodily samples. The prosecutor could not prove that curare was present, and Dr. Jascalevich was eventually acquitted.

There are several screening tests available. One commonly used test for drugs in urine is the enzyme multiplied immunoassay technique (EMIT). This test is based on an immunological principle of antibody-antigen reaction. An **antibody** to the drug (**antigen**) being tested for is added to the urine sample. Also added to the sample is a known amount of the drug being analyzed with an enzyme attached to it, so that enzymatic activity can be measured. If the urine sample contains a large amount of drug, the drug will bind to the antibody and, by competition, prevent binding of the enzyme-drug complex to the antibody. Thus, more of the free enzyme can be measured. If little drug is present in the urine sample, then more of the enzyme-drug complex will bind to the antibody, and enzyme activity will be less. The more drug in a person's urine, the greater the amount of measurable enzyme activity. There are many variations of this antibody-antigen type testing. Since chemicals or metabolites of drugs with structures similar to the drug of interest may cross-react with the antibody and falsely indicate a positive result (a false positive), this test is considered a screening test. Subsequent tests must be done to positively identify the chemical in the urine sample and to determine its concentration. If something in the sample prevents the drug from reacting with the antibody, the result would appear negative (a false negative). Although the EMIT test cannot determine accurately the amount of chemical present, the analysis is very sensitive and can detect quantities of drug in the nanogram (ng) range, one-billionth of a gram or 1×10^{-9} gram.

Another screening procedure for detecting drugs is based on the drug reacting with a reagent to produce a characteristic color. Color tests are simple and quick and require small amounts of sample. Items found at a crime scene may be analyzed for the presence of drugs and urine samples and tissue extracts may be screened for some drugs using color tests. Any positive result must be confirmed using gas chromatography (GC), gas chromatography/mass spectrometry (GC/MS), high-performance liquid chromatography (HPLC), or infrared spectrometry.

CHROMATOGRAPHY

The application of chromatography is widely used for detecting drugs. Chromatography can separate a mixture of chemicals from one another so that each can be identified and quantified. The principle of separation is based on the fact that different chemicals have different affinities for a particular material, and each chemical can be released more or less easily than the other from that material. Thus, there are two phases in a chromatographic system, a stationary phase to which the chemicals adhere and a mobile phase that passes over the stationary phase and takes with it the released chemical.

Gas chromatography (GC) uses a thin column made of stainless steel or glass. The stationary phase is a liquid such as methyl silicone or a solid such as silica, and the mobile phase is a gas, usually helium or nitrogen. As the mobile phase moves along the stationary phase, volatile chemicals, depending on the heat of the column, leave the stationary phase and travel in the mobile phase to the end of the column, where a detector is located. Chemicals with lesser affinity for the stationary phase are released before those with greater affinity. As each chemical reaches the end, the detector sends a signal to a recorder. The time it takes for a chemical to reach the detector from the time the sample is placed in the column is termed the retention time. Chemicals are identified by their retention time for a given separation system.

If liquid were used instead of gas for the mobile phase, this procedure would be termed high-performance liquid chromatography (HPLC or LC). Volatile chemicals are more easily separated using GC, while chemicals in solution are separated using HPLC (Figure 3.2).

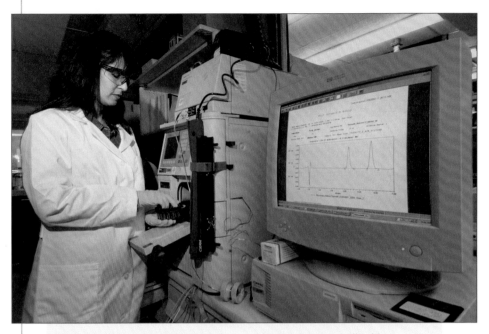

FIGURE 3.2 A scientist prepares a high-performance liquid chromatography (HPLC) machine to analyze a blood sample. The results of the test are visualized on the monitor to her right.

While retention time might be helpful in identifying a chemical, it may not be accurate enough, and an additional technique must be applied to confirm the chemical's identity. The gas and chemical exit the GC and flow into an attached instrument called a mass spectrometer (MS). Inside the MS, electrons or chemicals bombard the chemical in the gas, resulting in its fragmentation into smaller pieces of varying molecular weights. Here, each chemical is broken down into various size fragments, with the total group of fragments representing a specific chemical, much like a fingerprint. Thus far, no two chemicals have produced the same fragment pattern. The fragments pass through an electric or magnetic field and are separated according to the mass of the fragment. The spectrum of fragments is compared to thousands of spectra in a library of chemicals and is identified. A known amount of pure chemical is tested, and the results are then compared with the unknown sample to be certain of the identification and to allow quantification. The gas chromatography/mass spectrometry (GC/MS) technique is very sensitive, and can detect chemicals in the nanogram (ng) range. Results obtained by GC/MS are considered confirmatory.

Screening and confirmatory tests have cutoff values. The values for drugs of abuse are provided in Table 3.1. These values are based on various factors, including the precision and accuracy of the individual test systems. If the test result is higher than the cutoff value, the result is presumed positive; if it is lower, the result is presumed negative. This does not mean that the drug is totally absent, only that its concentration is below the cutoff value. It may become important for a particular case to determine using other assays whether the drug is, in fact, present at any level.

Thin layer chromatography (TLC) uses the same principles as GC or HPLC but is performed on a glass plate containing an adsorbent, such as silica or alumina, that attracts other molecules to its surface. A small portion of the sample to be analyzed is spotted on the plate. The plate is placed upright in a tank containing a small amount of solvent that then rises up the plate and separates the components of the sample. The separated components can be located with an ultraviolet lamp or by spraying the plate with chemicals to produce color.

Capillary electrophoresis, a relatively new technique, uses an electric current to separate compounds based on their size, charge, and mobile phase solubility. This technique requires small amounts of sample. An analytical technique that provides enhanced specificity and sensitivity for detection of chemicals is LC/MS/MS. This technique separates compounds by HPLC and then uses the MS to fragment the separated compounds. Unlike

Table 3.1 Cutoff Values for Urine Drug Tests[a]

Drug	FEDERAL[b]		NON-FEDERAL[c]	
	Screening[d]	Confirmatory[e]	Screening	Confirmatory
Cannabinoids	50		50	
Δ^9-tetrahydro-cannabinol-9-COOH[f]		15		15
Benzoylecgonine[g]	300	150	300	150
Phencyclidine	25	25	25	25
Amphetamines	1,000		1,000	
Opiates	2,000[h]		300	
Morphine		2,000[i]		300
Codeine		2,000		300
Benzodiazepines			300	300
Barbiturates			300	300
Methadone			300	300
Methaqualone			75	75
Propoxyphene			300	300
Alcohol			0.02%	0.02%[j]

[a] All values are expressed as ng/ml except alcohol, which is expressed as grams/100 ml.

[b] DHHS mandatory standards for federal agencies monitor only for five major drugs of abuse. All laboratories are certified and use the same cutoff values as regulated by SAMHSA. See 49CFR40.87.

[c] Local nonregulated testing for law enforcement (driving while impaired) or random drug test (employment, parole, child custody, sports, drug rehabilitation). These values may differ among commercial laboratories; average values are presented.

[d] Testing by immunoassay.

[e] Testing by GC/MS.

[f] Metabolite of marijuana.

[g] Metabolite of cocaine.

[h] Federal standards were set higher to account for the possibility that poppy seed foods had been ingested.

[i] A morphine level of 2000 ng/ml or more requires a test for 6-monoacetylmorphine (6-MAM, heroin metabolite) with a cutoff at 10 ng/ml.

[j] Testing by gas chromatography.

single MS analysis, however, some fragments are selected and then further fragmented.

Samples that contain volatile chemicals at room temperature are analyzed differently. A closed container with blood at room temperature will have volatile chemicals in the airspace above the blood sample. A definite volume of air above the sample of blood is drawn into a syringe and injected into a chromatograph. For each volatile chemical, there is a definite ratio of the concentration of chemical above the liquid phase relative to the concentration in the liquid phase at a given temperature. (This principle is known as Henry's law.) Thus, determining the amount of chemical in the sample taken above the liquid allows calculation of the amount in the liquid. This technique, known as headspace gas chromatography, is valuable for determining levels of ethyl alcohol, aldehydes, ketones, petroleum distillates, halogenated hydrocarbons, and gases such as nitrous oxide, methane, and freon.

DETERMINING BLOOD ALCOHOL CONCENTRATION

Blood alcohol concentration (BAC) is often based not on an actual sample of blood but rather on the concentration of alcohol in a sample of breath (Figure 3.3). Alcohol is volatile, and, as described by Henry's law, there is a constant relationship between the amount of alcohol vapor found in a volume of air (breath sample) and the amount of alcohol found in a volume of liquid (blood). All breath-testing equipment uses the blood-breath ratio of 2,100:1 for alcohol. This means that the amount of alcohol found in 2,100 milliliters of breath is equivalent to the amount of alcohol found in 1 milliliters of blood.

This ratio may vary from individual to individual and, under certain conditions, even within the same individual. Determination of a BAC from a breath sample may not always be accurate, and this is often a point of argument in the courtroom.

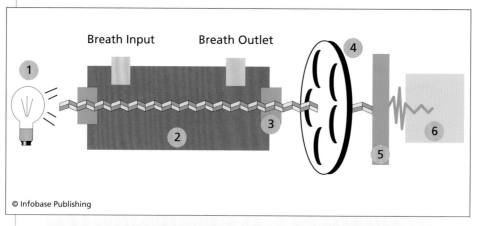

Breath Input   Breath Outlet

© Infobase Publishing

FIGURE 3.3 A breathalyzer measures the amount of infrared (IR) energy absorbed by alcohol molecules. In this illustration, IR energy from a lamp (1) travels through a chamber (2) holding the subject's breath. As the IR energy exits the chamber, it is focused by a lens (3), passed through IR filters (4), and then converted into electrical signals (5). A computer (6) receives the electrical signals and computes the blood alcohol concentration.

The new automated breath-testing instruments use infrared technology. Different chemicals absorb different amounts of energy at different frequencies of the electromagnetic spectrum. The electromagnetic spectrum ranges from large-wavelength radio waves to small-wavelength gamma rays. Infrared radiation, which is not visible to the human eye, has wavelengths slightly longer than red, the last color of our visible rainbow. At the other end of the rainbow is the color violet. Just below violet, again not visible to the human eye, is ultraviolet. When a breath sample is analyzed, the sample is irradiated with specific infrared wavelengths, and the chemicals in the breath absorb some of the energy. Based on the amount of energy transmitted from one end of the instrument and the amount detected at the other end of the instrument, one can determine the amount of energy absorbed and thereby the concentrations of alcohol present. Since other substances in the breath may also absorb energy, although in amounts different than alcohol at the different wavelengths, the instrument is calibrated at several wavelengths to take into account these interfering substances.

Once a drug has been identified and its concentration determined, the forensic scientist might be able to form an opinion as to whether a causal relationship exists between drug and the incident under investigation. If the concentration is too low to conclude causality, other explanations for the event may be sought. The forensic scientist has available vast amounts of literature to assist in making this determination. The forensic scientist

Drug Recognition Experts

Alcohol is not the only chemical that causes one to become impaired and drive erratically. Any chemical that affects mental functions, including some common prescription drugs as well as controlled substances, can impair the ability to drive.

In the 1980s, a new program was instituted to certify police officers as Drug Recognition Experts (DRE). DREs conduct a 12-step evaluation test that enables the officers to determine whether an individual is under the influence of alcohol or other drugs and determine the type of drug causing the impairment. The 12 steps include a breath test for the presence of alcohol; a discussion with the arresting officer; a preliminary examination of the eyes to determine pupil size and a measurement of the pulse; an examination of the eyes for involuntary movement, or **nystagmus**, and convergence; an evaluation of the four psychophysical divided attention examinations (the

(continues)

(continued from page 37)

one-leg stand test, the walk-and-turn test, the finger-to-nose test, and the Romberg balance test); a measurement of blood pressure, body temperature, and a second measure of the pulse; a darkroom examination of pupil size and reaction; a test of muscle tone; an examination of the skin for injection sites; the noting of any statements made by the suspect; the noting of the DRE's opinion as to whether the suspect is under the influence of drugs and, if so, which one; and, finally, obtaining a blood or urine sample.[2]

The tests are designed to predict which of seven categories of drug the suspect may have used: (1) CNS depressants, (2) CNS stimulants, (3) cannabinoids, (4) phencyclidine, (5) opioids, (6) hallucinogens, and (7) inhalants. The combination of results from the laboratory analysis of the blood or urine sample and from the 12-step evaluation test will help decide whether the defendant was impaired at the time of the stop.

can also add to the literature by publishing results from unusual and interesting cases. Forensic scientists often belong to one or more scientific associations and attend meetings where ideas are exchanged and new information is presented.

There are two main groups that accredit forensic laboratories: the governmental National Institute on Drug Abuse (NIDA) and the nongovernmental American Society of Crime Laboratory Directors (ASCLAD). Accreditation by the former is required for the laboratory to perform workplace testing for federal agencies. The groups monitor personnel training and development, record keeping, evidence control, quality control, and, most importantly, proficiency testing, which helps ensure the accuracy of the scientists and of the laboratory procedures.

SUMMARY

Drugs can be identified and their concentrations quantified using a variety of techniques. Some of the techniques screen the unknown sample to narrow the number of possible drug categories. The techniques of chromatography and mass spectrometry are used routinely for identification and quantification of chemicals. Quantitation of drug in biological samples is important to establish a causal relationship between drug and effect. Various biological samples can be analyzed, but blood is best for establishing causal relationships. Urine testing can indicate prior use of the drug but has limited value in establishing causality. A drug recognition expert (DRE) is trained to examine people and, based on a battery of tests, determine whether an individual is under the influence of a particular drug.

Drug Abuse and Teenager Statistics

An individual might begin using drugs to diminish anxiety and avoid dealing with problems, or to experience euphoria. Drugs used for their euphoric effect are sometimes termed **recreational drugs**. Use of such drugs often involves development of **physical** and/or **psychological dependence**. Psychological dependence is loss of control regarding drug use for either its positive effects or to avoid negative effects when the drug is unavailable. For example, an individual may make several unsuccessful attempts to stop using drugs and/or spend much time and effort in obtaining drugs. These are also signs of physical dependence, which additionally involves developing **tolerance**, a decreased sensitivity to the drug, and exhibiting withdrawal symptoms if the drug is not available.

Tolerance can develop in two ways. In pharmacokinetic tolerance, the drug is metabolized more quickly, thereby lowering the blood levels. In pharmacodynamic tolerance, cells adapt to the presence of the drug and are no longer affected at the usual concentration. Either way, higher doses of the drug are required to achieve a certain effect. When tolerance develops to pharmacologically similar drugs, this is termed **cross-tolerance**, and one drug may substitute for another. Some drugs of abuse are more likely to cause psychological dependence, while others cause both types of dependence. The word *addiction* is sometimes used to describe these states of dependence along with compulsive drug use.

If the user is drug dependent and does not get enough drug to satisfy his or her craving, withdrawal begins to set in. With some drugs, withdrawal is a very painful experience. Signs and symptoms may include depression, aggression, restlessness, irritability, headache, chills, vomiting, sweating, and painful jerking muscle reactions. To avoid these symptoms, people usually will do whatever it takes to get more drugs. With opioids, for example, where it is necessary to take drugs every few hours, such extreme needs may lead to criminal activity to sustain the drug habit.

Many drugs of abuse make the individual feel excited, aroused, and strong. Others result in drowsiness and poor coordination. Coupled with these feelings, however, may be an impairment of cognitive functions such as judgment, perception, and attentiveness. When these effects are combined, the individual may make rash decisions and take risks that otherwise would not be undertaken, which can lead to motor vehicle accidents and criminal activities such as robbery and homicide.

Often, when tissue or fluid samples from individuals under the influence of drugs are analyzed, more than one drug is present. Taking different drugs of abuse at the same time is particularly dangerous because of drug interaction. For example, many drugs of abuse are central nervous system depressants. While each drug may not completely arrest respiration, the combination of drugs may. Many drugs of abuse increase blood pressure and, taken in combination, might lead to a stroke.

Injecting drugs of abuse presents special hazards. Transmission of the AIDS or hepatitis virus occurs often by using "dirty" needles, that is, needles with another user's blood on them. Also, many drugs contain other substances such as **adulterants** or

diluents. These other substances may not completely dissolve when added to water, and injection of tiny particles may clog blood vessels. Commonly added agents that may be found during analysis of fluids and tissues include caffeine, acetaminophen (Tylenol®), and phenobarbital, a sedative.

In 1970, in response to a rising level of drug abuse, Congress enacted the Comprehensive Drug Abuse Prevention and Control Act, also known as the Controlled Substances Act (CSA). The Drug Enforcement Administration has categorized controlled substances (based on the CSA) into five different schedules.[3] The five schedules are defined as follows:

Schedule I: Substances with no accepted medicinal use in the United States and a high potential for abuse; for example, heroin, marijuana, lysergic acid diethylamide (LSD), mescaline, and psilocybin.

Schedule II: Substances with a medicinal use but also a high potential for psychological or physical dependence. A written prescription is required for use; for example, morphine, cocaine, and oxycodone.

Schedule III: Substances with less potential for abuse than drugs in Schedule I or II; for example, methylphenidate, amphetamine, secobarbital, and anabolic steroids.

Schedule IV: Substances with low abuse potential; for example, some barbiturate compounds, chloral hydrate, and benzodiazepine derivatives.

Schedule V: Substances with limited potential for abuse; for example, some codeine preparations for cough, and Lomotil® (which contains the opioid diphenoxylate) for diarrhea.

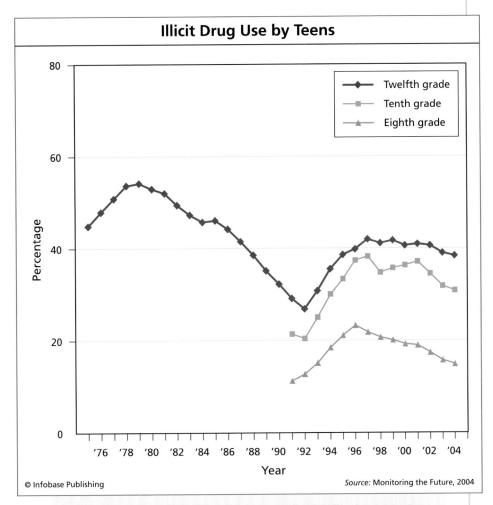

Illicit Drug Use by Teens

— Twelfth grade
— Tenth grade
— Eighth grade

© Infobase Publishing

Source: Monitoring the Future, 2004

FIGURE 4.1 The 2004 Monitoring the Future (MTF) survey reveals that use of any kind of illicit drug peaked in the early 1980s, decreased over the next 10 to 15 years, but then began to increase in the mid-1990s.[4]

To circumvent restrictions under the CSA, people began to synthesize drugs that are chemically and pharmacologically similar to those listed in Schedules I to V. These are termed **designer drugs**. To control the distribution of such chemicals, Congress amended the CSA in 1986 by passing the Controlled Substance Analogue Enforcement Act.

DRUG USE AND ABUSE IN ADOLESCENTS

Adolescent substance abuse has been a major health issue for many years. Governmental and other agencies survey the use of drugs of abuse by teenagers for each drug according to school grade, age, gender, and ethnicity. Results obtained from such surveys, and from reports of emergency room visits, arrest data, and accidents, provide information to monitor trends in abuse of illicit and non-illicit dependence-producing substances by teenagers (Figure 4.1).

The extent of drug use in 2003 for different drugs is presented in Table 4.1. According to the 2003 National Survey on Drug Use and Health (NSDUH), 11.2% of 12- to 17-year-olds reported current use of illicit drugs, 30.5% reported use at least once during their lifetime, and 21.8% reported use within the past year.[5]

According to the Drug Abuse Warning Network (DAWN), a public health surveillance system, in the second half of 2003, there were 627,923 drug-related visits to the emergency rooms of hospitals. Of these visits, 141,343 involved alcohol alone or alcohol along with other drugs. Of all the alcohol-related visits, 16,770 were made by 12-to 17-year olds in a ratio of about 2:1, males to females.[6]

Drug use by teenagers in 2004 appears to have declined, though use of inhalants and oxycodone (OxyContin®), a prescription opioid pain reliever, are on the rise.[7] Recent reports indicate that a ready source of drugs of abuse for adolescents is prescription drugs found in the home medicine cabinet, as well as prescription drugs available on the Internet.[8]

FORENSIC ISSUES

In cases involving motor vehicles, the defendant generally tries to disprove the claim that the concentration of drug found in blood could have affected driving performance, or argues that a finding of drug in urine only indicates drug use prior to the accident but has no value in proving a causal link to impaired driving.

In many states, it is illegal to drive with any detectable amount of controlled substance in blood. Other states define "drugged driving" as driving when the driver is incapable of driving safely

Table 4.1 Percent of 12- to 17- Year-Olds Reporting Drug Use in 2003			
Drug Type	Lifetime	Past Year	Past Month
Any Illicit Drug	30.5%	21.8%	11.2%
Marijuana/hashish	19.6	15.0	7.9
Cocaine	2.6	1.8	0.6
Crack	0.6	0.4	0.1
Heroin	0.3	0.1	0.1
Hallucinogens	5.0	3.1	1.0
LSD	1.6	0.6	0.2
PCP	0.8	0.4	0.1
Ecstasy	2.4	1.3	0.4
Inhalants	10.7	4.5	1.3
Methamphetamine	1.3	0.7	0.3

or is impaired. According to a 2003 NSDUH survey, 10.9 million people drove under the influence of drugs in the prior year. Of young adults aged 18 to 25 years, 14.1% drove after using drugs. Studies of impaired drivers, crash victims, and fatalities revealed marijuana to be the most prevalent drug used. In the United States in 2003, there were 2,283 alcohol-related motor vehicle fatalities among 15- to 20-year-olds.[9] In 2004, 12.7% of high school seniors drove after using marijuana.[10]

According to the Federal Bureau of Investigation's Crime in the United States report, during 2003 there were 137,658 juveniles arrested by law enforcement agencies for drug abuse violations.

Monitoring Drug Abuse Among Teenagers

There are many different governmental agencies that monitor the use of drugs by teenagers. One of the largest, the National Institute on Drug Abuse (NIDA), sets scientific standards in drug testing, maintains Web sites for teenagers with useful information about drug effects, and funds the Monitoring the Future (MTF) program conducted by the University of Michigan. Beginning in 1975, MTF monitored drug use among twelfth graders, and in 1991 expanded their studies to include eighth and tenth graders. Data collected include usage in the past 30 days, in the past year, and lifetime usage. The Drug Abuse Warning Network (DAWN), under the supervision of the Substance Abuse and Mental Health Services Administration (SAMHSA), monitors drug-related visits to emergency departments and deaths investigated by medical examiners. One report, the National Survey on Drug Use and Health (NSDUH), surveys individuals 12 years or older to determine

During fiscal year 2002, the Drug Enforcement Administration (DEA) arrested 675 persons under the age of 19 involved with cocaine, marijuana, methamphetamine, or opioids. According to another study, a median of 59.7% of male juvenile detainees and 45.9% of female juvenile detainees tested positive for drug use in 2002.[11]

SUMMARY

Drugs of abuse can induce physical and psychological dependence and impair cognitive functions. Individuals who use

their use of alcohol or illicit drugs in the prior year and whether they drove under the influence of such drugs. Another report, the Drug and Alcohol Services Information System (DASIS), monitors treatment programs for drug abuse. The Office of National Drug Control Policy, under the White House Drug Policy program, establishes policies and priorities for the United States and provides information concerning drug use and effects. Many of the agencies provide reports of the data collected in various formats analyzed by drug, age, gender, and race. Some of the reports are available on the Internet. The National Institute of Justice conducts surveys of drug use among arrested individuals under its Arrestee Drug Abuse Monitoring (ADAM) program. The Centers for Disease Control and Prevention (CDC) monitors ninth to twelfth graders for behaviors that impose health risks under its Youth Risk Behavior Surveillance System (YRBSS).

drugs may make rash decisions or take risks that can result in violence and accidents. The use of drugs of abuse by teenagers is well documented. Many governmental agencies monitor the use of drugs, the presence of drugs in accidents, and the number of drug-related emergency department admissions. Recent surveys indicate that while overall drug use by adolescents decreased in the period from the 1980s to mid-1990s, it began to rise after that. Even with a decrease in drug use, a significant number of young adults use or have used drugs and have driven while under the influence of drugs.

Cannabinoids

5

Cannabinoids are isolated from the plant _Cannabis sativa_, which was initially found in Central Asia. Marijuana refers to any part of the cannabis plant that can induce **psychotomimetic** effects, a loss of contact with reality. Marijuana induces a wide spectrum of behavioral effects and has been classified as a stimulant, sedative, or **hallucinogen**. Marijuana is the most widely used illicit drug in the United States. There are more than 200 slang terms for marijuana, including bhang, blunt, bud, dope, gangster, grass, herb, jive, joint, Mary Jane, pot, reefer, roach, rope, skunk, Thai stick, weed, and zig zag man. Marijuana has also been used in combination with codeine cough syrup or with embalming fluid.

Cannabinoids have been used for over 4,000 years as a sedative, a remedy for relief of pain, epilepsy, and asthma, and in religious ceremonies. The Spanish brought _Cannabis sativa_ to the Americas, and Mexican laborers introduced the drug into the southern portion of the United States around 1910. The plant has been used for its fiber (called hemp) content for over 2,000 years. Early American settlers grew the plant for its hemp content, and the Marijuana Tax Act of 1937 banned cultivation, possession, and distribution of hemp plants except for making cord and twine.

Marijuana contains 421 different chemicals, including 61 cannabinoids. The potency is based on the percentage of the active ingredient delta-9-tetrahydrocannabinol (THC) per dry weight (Figure 5.1). Preparations from leaves and flowers contain about 3% THC, sinsemilla (the unpollinated seedless female plant) contains about 5% THC, hashish (resin from the flower tops of female plants) contains approximately 10% THC, and hashish oil, a viscous product obtained by extracting the resin with solvent, may contain as much as 20% THC. The word *hashish* comes from the Arabic word meaning "grass." Street names for hashish include charas, gangster, ganja, hash, and hemp. In 1965, Israeli

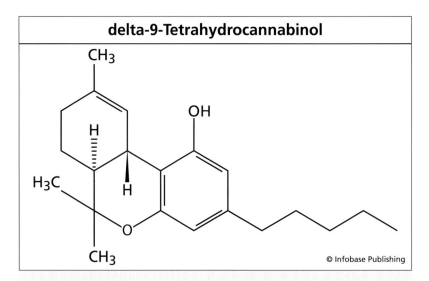

FIGURE 5.1 THC, also known as delta-9-tetrahydrocannabinol, is the main psychoactive chemical in the cannabis plant. Its chemical formula is $C_{21}H_{30}O_2$.

Medical Marijuana Usage in California

On November 5, 1996, the people of California passed Proposition 215 (The California Compassionate Use Act of 1996, CA Health and Safety Code Section 11362.5) by 56% of the vote. It provides that if recommended by a physician, a primary caregiver (an individual designated as being responsible for the housing, health, or safety of the patient) who obtains and uses marijuana for medical purposes is not subject to criminal prosecution or sanction. The proposition also removes state-level criminal penalties on the use, possession, and cultivation of marijuana by patients who possess a written or oral recommendation from their physician. Medical conditions typically covered by the law include, but are not limited to, arthritis, anorexia, cancer, chronic pain, glaucoma, HIV or AIDS, migraine, and multiple sclerosis. The California Legislature adopted guidelines in 2003 outlining how much medicinal marijuana patients may grow and possess. Under the guidelines, patients and/or their primary caregivers may possess no more than 8 ounces of dried marijuana and/or 6 mature (or 12 immature) marijuana plants. However, patients may possess larger amounts if recommended by a physician.[12] Eleven other states have passed similar laws. On June 6, 2005, the United States Supreme Court ruled that state laws do not protect against federal laws banning use of marijuana. The federal government, therefore, can still prosecute sick people using marijuana in a state that allows it. The Supreme Court ruled that it is up to Congress to change the laws allowing marijuana use for medical reasons.

scientists R. Mechoulam and Y. Gaoni reported the isolation and synthesis of THC.

Marijuana, hashish, hashish oil, and THC are listed in Schedule I. However, marijuana has been used medically as an anti-emetic agent (an agent that decreases or stops vomiting) for patients receiving cancer chemotherapy, to decrease intraocular pressure in patients with glaucoma, as an antispasmodic for treating multiple sclerosis, and as an appetite-enhancing drug to diminish wasting in individuals with AIDS. Marinol® (dronabinol) is a synthetic THC that is taken orally in capsules containing amounts of THC up to 10 milligrams. It has been approved for medical use in the United States since 1986 and is a Schedule III drug.

PHARMACOLOGY OF MARIJUANA

Marijuana is usually smoked in the form of a cigarette (a "joint") consisting of chopped-up leaves and stems, or smoked from a pipe or a water pipe. Much of the THC is destroyed by heat during smoking. The effects of THC are felt within minutes and last from two to five hours.

Marijuana may also be eaten (baked into cookies or brownies), brewed in tea, or swallowed in pill form. Much of oral THC is destroyed in the stomach, and more is destroyed via first-pass metabolism. THC is metabolized primarily in the liver to an active metabolite, 11-hydroxy-THC (11-OH-THC), that is further converted to the inactive carboxylated compound 11-nor-delta 9-THC-9-COOH (THC-COOH) and its glucuronide form. It is these metabolites that are tested for in urine samples.

THC is lipid soluble and is released slowly from fatty tissue. This explains why cannabinoid metabolites may be detected for 3 to 10 days in occasional users and for many weeks in chronic users, even after drug use has stopped. Changes in activity or diet that release fat from fat cells may increase the level of cannabinoids detected in urine. THC crosses the placental membranes, and possible effects on the fetus or infant include a delay in maturation, an alteration of the gestational period, low birth weight, and behavioral changes. THC is also found in breast milk.

Marijuana acts on cannabinoid receptors found in brain and peripheral tissues. A natural brain chemical, anandamide, can also activate the receptors. Marijuana has a range of behavioral effects, including feelings of euphoria, relaxation, mood changes, panic reactions, and paranoia. It also causes an altered time perception, lack of concentration, and impairs judgment, learning, and memory. If alone, a person may become quiet and drowsy, but if with a group of people, a person may become very outgoing and laugh easily. Other changes include **psychosis**, delusions, and hallucinations. Though controversial, the term "amotivational syndrome" is used to describe young people who drop out of social and school activities because of marijuana usage.

The physiological effects of marijuana include increased heart rate, dryness of the mouth and throat, increased appetite, enlargement of the blood vessels and pupils, sleepiness, decreased respiration rate, and psychomotor impairment (Figure 5.2). **Ataxia** (unsteady balance) and bloodshot eyes are characteristic of marijuana intoxication. Use of marijuana over a long period of time can cause lung damage, impairment of cognitive function, alteration of the immune system, reduced testosterone levels and enlarged breast tissue in males, and **schizophrenia**, a mental disorder that results in disorganized behavior and social withdrawal. Tolerance does develop, but there is no strong evidence that marijuana causes physical dependence. Stopping marijuana after prolonged use, however, can lead to restlessness, irritability, insomnia, nausea, anxiety, depression, and anorexia.

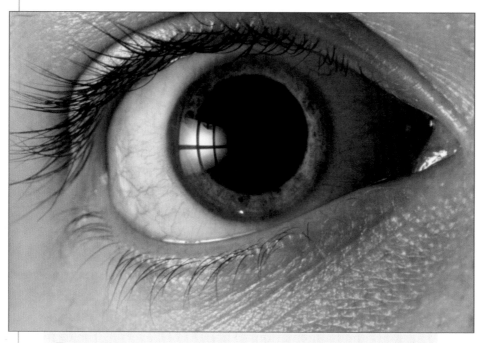

FIGURE 5.2   A close-up of a human eye with a dilated pupil is shown in the photograph above. Dilation of the pupil (mydriasis) occurs in response to release of adrenaline in the body (the fight-or-flight response) or the use of drugs such as amphetamine or marijuana.

FORENSIC ISSUES

Hemp seed oil, legally sold in the United States, is a source for essential omega fatty acids. This product is made from sterilized seeds that cannot grow new marijuana plants. Although the small amount of marijuana present cannot exert a euphoric effect, sufficient amounts of THC metabolites are produced and can be detected in urine. A positive result can be explained away if it can be proven that the individual had used hemp seed oil. Hemp seeds are also being used in a variety of foods such as chips and granola. Another complication in drug testing arises with the issue of secondhand smoke. Under certain conditions, inhalation of secondhand smoke contains sufficient amounts of THC to register positive on a urine drug test.

Seized samples of marijuana are analyzed in the laboratory using a color test, thin-layer chromatography, and a microscopic test. The Duquenois-Levine color test, although not specific for marijuana, is often used. Using the microscope one can see on the upper side of the marijuana leaf characteristic "bear claw"-shaped cystolithic hairs, which contain calcium carbonate.

In driving-related court cases, it is often difficult to prove impairment, since even if the marijuana was used hours or days earlier, the metabolites are still being released from fat cells and excreted in urine. Defense arguments in cases with positive random urine tests include use of hemp seed oil, unknowingly ingesting marijuana-laced foods, or exposure to secondhand smoke. The latter argument is very dependent on the concentration of metabolite in urine.

In one particular case, a motorcyclist hit a car and was severely injured. At the hospital, approximately one hour after the accident, the cyclist's blood alcohol content (BAC) was 0.021%. Back extrapolation (see Chapter 7) to the time of the accident could increase that value to 0.036%. His urine tests revealed use of cocaine and marijuana. Marijuana metabolites were confirmed by gas chromatography/mass spectrometry (GC/MS). All these results were used to try and prove that the cyclist was impaired. However, the presence of drug in urine is not a good indicator of drug concentration in blood or of impairment at the time of the accident, and the BAC was probably too low to cause impairment. At best, one could say that the cyclist does use drugs and uses several of them at the same time, but use of the drugs may not have played a role in causing the accident. The case was settled.

SUMMARY

The active ingredient in marijuana is delta-9-tetrahydrocannabinol (THC). Marijuana may be smoked or ingested. THC is stored in fatty tissue, from which it is released slowly. THC can induce many behavioral and physiological changes, some dependent on the social setting. Chronic use can lead to serious effects on the endocrine, respiratory, immune, and nervous systems. Use of marijuana during pregnancy may lead to abnormal fetal development. Although tolerance to THC can develop, there is no strong evidence of physical dependence. THC is being used for medical purposes, and such use has sparked debate between law enforcement and the medical community.

Central Nervous System Stimulants

6

This chapter will focus on cocaine, amphetamine, methamphetamine, cathinone and methcathinone, and ephedrine—just a few of the many central nervous system (CNS) stimulants.

COCAINE

Cocaine, a Schedule II drug, is found in the leaf of the coca plant growing mostly in the Andean region of South America. The two main plant species are *Erythroxylum coca* and *Erythroxylum novogranatense*. The Indians of Peru used coca plant leaves for thousands of years as part of religious ceremonies and knew of its ability to abolish hunger and decrease fatigue. Cocaine was isolated from the plant in 1859 by the German chemist Albert Niemann (Figure 6.1). In 1863, it became popular as a component of the French wine, Vin Mariani, sold for its restorative and tonic properties. In 1884, Sigmund Freud wrote a paper about the effects of cocaine and described its ability to enhance elation, physical endurance, and mental agility. Also in 1884, the medical community learned of cocaine's local anesthetic properties. In 1886, in the United States, a pharmacist named

John Styth Pemberton prepared a drink containing extract of coca leaf and caffeine that he termed Coca-Cola. Today, because of drug laws enacted in the early 1900s, coca extract is still used to prepare Coca-Cola, but the cocaine is removed. Cocaine is used medicinally as a local anesthetic, applied topically by some surgeons for nasal, throat, and ear surgery.

Cocaine is found in several forms. It can be extracted from the coca leaf to form coca paste (basuco, pitillo), which is not water soluble but can be smoked. The paste can be further treated to form cocaine hydrochloride (cocaine powder), which can be dissolved in water and injected, or can be snorted into the nostril.

Freebase cocaine and crack cocaine, each containing cocaine base, are prepared from cocaine hydrochloride by adding ammonia and ether or sodium bicarbonate and heat, respectively. Applying heat to evaporate the ether can cause the ether to ignite, which can cause severe burns. In preparing crack cocaine, the

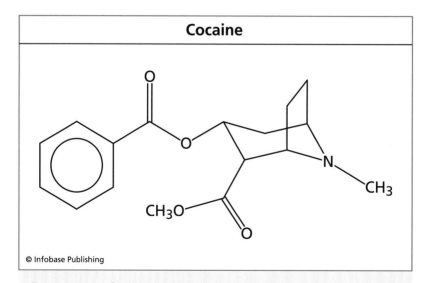

Cocaine

© Infobase Publishing

FIGURE 6.1 Cocaine is obtained from the leaves of the coca plant. It has a chemical formula of $C_{17}H_{21}NO_4$.

mixture is allowed to dry into a cake that is cut into little pieces. Cocaine, used as freebase or crack, is not water soluble and is smoked. When smoking the small crack pieces, carbon dioxide is released and makes a crackling sound, hence, the name crack. Any form of cocaine base is easily differentiated from cocaine hydrochloride using infrared spectrometry.

Some street names for cocaine include blow, C, Charlie, coke, crack, dynamite, happy dust, nose candy, rock, snow, snuff, stardust, toot, and white lady. The combination of cocaine and heroin is termed speedball.

AMPHETAMINE AND RELATED DRUGS

Amphetamine, a Schedule II drug, was synthesized by the German chemist L. Edeleano in 1887 (Figure 6.2). The trade names for amphetamine are Benzedrine and Dexedrine. Smith, Kline, and French marketed Benzedrine inhaler in the 1930s for respiratory disorders. Since amphetamine decreases drowsiness and fatigue, it is marketed for narcolepsy and attention-deficit/hyperactivity disorder (ADHD), and was used as an appetite suppressant (anorectic) in diet regimens. Amphetamine was supplied to the

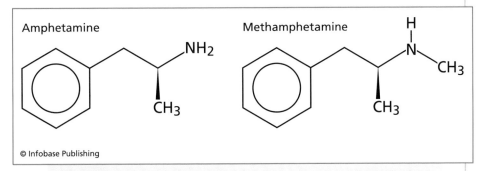

© Infobase Publishing

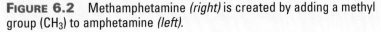

FIGURE 6.2 Methamphetamine *(right)* is created by adding a methyl group (CH_3) to amphetamine *(left)*.

soldiers during World War II to overcome fatigue, and to aviators in the Persian Gulf War. Recently, baseball has banned use of amphetamines. Street names for amphetamine include amp, black beauties, crosses, crystal, dexies, pep pills, speed, truck drivers, and uppers.

Methamphetamine, a Schedule II drug, was first synthesized in 1919. It can be synthesized from ephedrine or pseudoephedrine. Methamphetamine is available by prescription for weight control, ADHD, and narcolepsy under the brand name Desoxyn®. Street names for methamphetamine include chalk, crank, crystal, fire, glass, ice, rocks, shabu, speed, and yaba. Methamphetamine is often found at **rave** sites, where people exert themselves while dancing and deprive themselves of sleep, food, and drink, which can result in increased body temperature with excessive sweating and possibly a salt imbalance.

Cathinone is isolated from the leaves of khat, *Catha edulis*, a plant that grows in East Africa, Southern Arabia, and the Middle East, as well as in the desert areas of the southern United States (Figure 6.3). Cathinone has been used since the thirteenth century, when it was given to soldiers to relieve fatigue. The youngest leaves at the top of the plant are preferred. As the leaves dry, cathinone, which is structurally related to ephedrine and amphetamine, is converted to the less potent cathine. The synthesis of methcathinone, more potent than cathinone, became popular in Russia and was brought to the United States in the early 1990s. Methcathinone is easy to synthesize from ephedrine. Cathinone and methcathinone are Schedule I drugs, and cathine is a Schedule IV drug. Street names for khat (cathinone) include Abyssinian tea, African salad, chat, kat, qat, and shat. Methcathinone is known as bathtub speed, cadillac express, cat, gagers, go-fast, and wild cat.

Ephedrine is found in the ephedra plant (*Ephedra sinica*—the Chinese herb Ma Huang). It is used as a nasal decongestant

FIGURE 6.3 Above, khat stems have been wrapped in banana leaves to preserve their freshness. Khat is a plant native to Africa, whose stems and leaves are chewed for their euphoric, stimulant effect.

and bronchodilator in asthmatic patients and was once used in weight control programs. Its **analog**, pseudoephedrine, can be found in many cold remedy products including Comtrex®, Sudafed®, Benadryl-D®, Drixoral®, Claritin-D®, Tylenol® Sinus, and Vicks DayQuil® Sinus. Ephedrine is metabolized to phenylpropanolamine, and both ephedrine and phenylpropanolamine have been removed from the over-the-counter market because of apparent increases in blood pressure leading to strokes.

PHARMACOLOGY OF CNS STIMULANTS

Depending on the drug and its form, CNS stimulants are usually taken either orally as a solid or tea or by the chewing of leaves, by injection, by smoking, or by snorting. Injection directly into the bloodstream or inhalation of smoke into the lungs induces a very rapid onset of action. CNS stimulants induce their effects by increasing the synaptic concentrations of several neurotransmitters, particularly norepinephrine (noradrenaline), dopamine, and serotonin. They stimulate the release of neurotransmitters and block their reuptake.

Cocaine

Cocaine is a local vasoconstrictor, and snorting of cocaine intranasally reduces the amount of blood flow to the area, resulting in a reduced rate of drug absorption and slower onset of action. Often in cocaine abusers, the reduced blood supply to the nasal septum leads to the development of a perforation between the nasal passages. The effects of cocaine last approximately 40 minutes, while the effects of other stimulants usually last several hours, as each has a different half-life.

One of the primary metabolites of cocaine is the inactive benzoylecgonine. Cocaine, but not benzoylecgonine, passes the blood-brain barrier. Any benzoylecgonine in brain is from cocaine metabolism therein. The half-life of cocaine is about one hour, but the half-life of benzoylecgonine is about five to seven hours. Cocaine is excreted in urine for about 10 hours, while benzoylecgonine can be found in urine as soon as one hour after use and for about three days thereafter. Urine drug screens test for this metabolite. If benzoylecgonine is detected in urine, use of cocaine occurred within the past 72 hours. Cocaine has also been found in breast milk. It passes the placental barrier, and there is some evidence that it causes fetal abnormalities. When both cocaine and alcohol are used at the same time, the two are metabolically combined to form cocaethylene, a compound as active as cocaine but with a longer half-life. Even though alcohol may no longer be detected, finding cocaethylene suggests that the individual may have been under the influence of both substances at the same time.

Methamphetamine

Methamphetamine passes the blood-brain barrier better than amphetamine, and there is evidence that chronic use of meth-amphetamine can result in permanent damage to dopamine neurons. Both pass the placental barrier, and there is some evidence that abuse by a pregnant woman can result in fetal abnormalities. Methamphetamine is found in breast milk. The half-life of methamphetamine and amphetamine is about 10 to 13 hours. Some methamphetamine is metabolized to amphet-amine, and amphetamine-glucuronide can be detected in urine for about two days. About 50% of methamphetamine is excreted unchanged in the urine over two to three days.

Cathinone

After chewing khat leaves, it can take up to two hours to achieve peak levels of cathinone. The half-life is about 4.5 hours.

Cathinone is metabolized to norephedrine and norpseudo-ephedrine. Cathinone is found in breast milk. Babies of mothers who used khat have low birth weights. Methcathinone acts like methamphetamine, and effects last four to six hours.

Most of the CNS stimulants induce similar psychological effects, including euphoria, an increased sense of strength and self-confidence, and sexual arousal. After the euphoric effect, a **dysphoria** follows, in which the individual feels restless, anxious, and depressed, and wants to repeat the experience. The drugs adversely affect judgment and decision making, and impair psychomotor functions. Physiologically, they increase heart rate, blood pressure, body temperature, and respiratory rate. The drugs also affect visual acuity by causing dilated pupils. High doses can lead to seizures, strokes, and cardiac arrhythmia. The latter can lead to sudden death. Prolonged use can result in personality changes, psychosis, hallucinations, paranoia, fatigue, weight loss, tremors, and depression. Cocaine use creates the sensation that bugs are burrowing under the skin, and longtime users can damage their skin through scratching. Tolerance may develop more with amphetamines than with cocaine; withdrawal signs and symptoms include depression, lethargy, and anxiety and sleep disorders.

FORENSIC ISSUES

The presence of cocaine or benzoylecgonine in blood, urine, hair, or other tissues is indicative of cocaine usage. No other known substance can give rise to a false positive, and there are no legitimate excuses to account for a positive result. There are many reports of hospitalized infants and children with positive urine test results indicative of exposure to cocaine. The most likely route of exposure was secondhand smoke in homes where crack cocaine was used.

In murder cases, high blood levels of cocaine or metabolites have sometimes served to argue on the defendant's behalf. If a murdered person was shown to have used cocaine, the defendant could argue that the killing was done in self-defense. If the defendant was the one who had used cocaine, the defense attorneys could argue that the defendant did not have the mental ability to form intent for murder.

In one actual case, a man and his girlfriend had a fight, during which the girlfriend stabbed the man and he died. She was charged with murder. Toxicological analysis of bodily samples from the deceased revealed the presence of alcohol in both blood and brain at a concentration of 0.19%, and the presence of cocaine; benzoylecgonine, the metabolite of cocaine; and cocaethylene, the metabolite of alcohol plus cocaine. At trial, in support of an argument for self-defense, testimony emphasized the adverse effects of alcohol, cocaine, and cocaethylene on behavior and judgment. The woman was acquitted of murder.

In another case involving alcohol and cocaine, the defendant shot three police officers and was charged with attempted murder. The defendant claims that he had no memory of the events. Urine analysis indicated the use of cocaine. Testimony at trial emphasized the adverse effects of cocaine on behavior and on the inability to form intent to kill. In this case, however, the man was found guilty and sentenced to 60 years to life.

In actual cases involving random employee urine tests that were positive for cocaine metabolite, people have offered many different ways of explaining the test results. For example, one person proposed that cocaine was put in his medication capsules, another that cocaine was added to her drink at a party, another person claimed that she inhaled cocaine as secondhand smoke while looking for someone in a crack house, and a garbage collector claimed that garbage bags had ripped open and covered him with white powder. Other explanations offered in defense were that urine samples were mixed up at the collection center or there were other errors related to **chain-of-custody**, the sequence of steps from point of collection to the reporting of results. These arguments have almost never been successful, and the individuals have had to resign from employment.

A positive screening test result for amphetamines may be due to use of amphetamine or methamphetamine-containing prescription or over-the-counter drugs. For example, the drug Selegiline, which is used to treat Parkinson's disease, is metabolized to amphetamine and methamphetamine. The nasal decongestant pseudoephedrine can cross-react in the test and result in a false positive. In the latter case, the confirmatory test is for amphetamine.

FIGURE 6.4 Methamphetamine that is manufactured illegally is usually a crystalline solid known as crystal meth or crystal.

Vicks® vapor inhaler, a decongestant, contains l-metham-phetamine, listed on the container as levmetamfetamine. Use of this product results in only l-amphetamine appearing in urine. If d-amphetamine is detected in urine, it could only have come from using d-methamphetamine or d-amphetamine-containing legal or illegal drugs.

Many people prepare methamphetamine in their homes (Figure 6.4), placing both themselves and their families in peril. Oregon has already passed legislation requiring a prescription for any cold and allergy medication containing pseudoephedrine, the chemical used to make methamphetamine. Congress has passed a law requiring that pseudoephedrine-containing products be sold only from behind the pharmacy counter.

SUMMARY

Drugs that stimulate the CNS cause euphoria and an increased sense of self-confidence, strength, and sexual arousal. Physiological responses include an increase in heart rate, blood pressure, temperature, and respiratory rate. The drugs act predominantly by increasing the synaptic levels of dopamine and norepinephrine. This class of drugs induces predominantly psychological dependence rather than physical dependence. Withdrawal signs and symptoms consist of dysphoria and restlessness.

7 Central Nervous System Depressants

Central nervous system (CNS) depressants include alcohol, barbiturates, benzodiazepines, gamma-hydroxybutyrate (GHB), chloral hydrate, glutethimide, and methaqualone.

THE HISTORY OF DEPRESSANTS

There is evidence that the Greeks, Egyptians, Hebrews, Japanese, Chinese, and Russians made alcoholic beverages thousands of years ago. Alcohol (ethanol, ethyl alcohol, and grain alcohol) is produced by yeast fermentation of sugar in fruits and grains to make wine, beer, or a variety of alcoholic spirits, including gin, vodka, and scotch.

The German chemist Adolph Von Bayer prepared barbiturates in the 1860s. The first barbiturate, barbital (Veronal), was marketed in 1903, and phenobarbital (Figure 7.1) was introduced in 1912. Barbiturates used to be common drugs of abuse in the 1950s and 1960s, but because of their dependence-inducing properties and association with suicides and accidental deaths, their use has been reduced significantly.

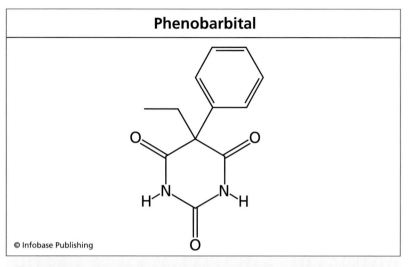

Phenobarbital

© Infobase Publishing

FIGURE 7.1 Phenobarbital is a barbiturate with the chemical formula $C_{12}H_{12}N_2O_3$.

In the 1930s, Dr. Leo Sternbach discovered benzodiazepines, and in 1954, he developed Librium, the first "tranquilizer," an ambiguous term that is no longer used. Though many people suffered serious side effects and developed drug dependence to benzodiazepines, these problems were not openly acknowledged until the late 1970s. Benzodiazepines are still the most commonly prescribed mood altering drugs, seen as alternatives to barbiturates to treat anxiety, muscle tension, and sleep disorders.

Dr. Henri Laborit synthesized gamma-hydroxybutyrate (GHB) in France in 1960 for use as an anesthetic, based on its chemical similarity to gamma-aminobutyric acid (GABA). Since it does not block out pain, use of GHB did not become widespread. It was discovered in the late 1970s that GHB could stimulate the release of growth hormone, and, although controversial, body builders and weight lifters began using it with the goal of reducing fat and increasing muscle mass.

PHARMACOLOGY OF CNS DEPRESSANTS

CNS depressants inhibit nerve activity, leading to decreased anxiety, sedation, uncoordinated movements, and, if the dose is high enough, unconsciousness and even death. Sometimes, however, the inhibition of nerve activity occurs in a pathway that normally inhibits our actions, causing the opposite effect of disinhibition, in which intoxicated people say and do things they normally would not.

Alcohol

Alcohol, taken orally, is absorbed in the stomach but mostly from the small intestine into the bloodstream. It first reaches the liver, where some alcohol is immediately metabolized (first-pass metabolism) by the enzyme alcohol dehydrogenase. Alcohol is a water-soluble chemical and distributes throughout body fluids but not readily into body fat. Females, who naturally have more lipid (fat) tissue per pound of mass, will have a higher BAC than males after consuming the same amount of alcohol.

There are 9.6 grams of alcohol in 1 ounce (30ml) of 80-proof (40% alcohol) hard liquor, 13.4 grams of alcohol in one 12-ounce can of beer (average alcohol content of 4.67%), and 11.4 grams of alcohol in a 4-ounce glass of wine (average alcohol content of 12%). A 150-pound male who consumes one can of beer over a short time period will have a BAC of approximately 0.029%. A 150-pound female who consumes one can of beer over the same time period will have a BAC of approximately 0.036%.

Though the rates of metabolism and excretion of many drugs are measured in terms of half-lives, the elimination of alcohol primarily by liver enzymes occurs as a constant amount per time regardless of its concentration. On average, the BAC decreases 0.015% per hour. Thus, it would take about five hours before someone's BAC reached zero if he or she consumed enough alcohol to have reached a BAC of 0.075%. Also, if one consumed only one drink per hour, it would require many hours before a significant BAC would accumulate. Since alcohol is volatile, some is excreted via the breath with each exhalation. This is the basis for the breath test (see Chapter 3). Alcohol is also excreted in urine, saliva, and sweat.

There is a relationship between BAC and alcohol's effects. Basically, a BAC of up to 0.05% results in little impairment, but with a BAC between 0.05% and 0.10%, some impairment of cognitive functions, such as attention span, information processing, and judgment, is seen. The individual begins to feel euphoric, talkative, show increased confidence, and exhibit a loss of inhibitions. There is a loss of fine motor coordination. Alcohol also inhibits the release of antidiuretic hormone from the pituitary gland. This causes diuresis, and explains the necessity of having to urinate after consuming alcoholic beverages. A BAC over 0.10% usually causes ataxia (unsteady balance), slurred speech, impaired memory, comprehension, and perception, and vomiting. Alcohol-induced blackouts, that is, a total amnesia of events that can never be recalled, usually occur at a BAC of around 0.28%. As alcohol is metabolized and eliminated, the individual returns to a normal state. Large enough doses can produce stupor, coma, and death.

Alcohol is toxic to the liver, and prolonged use results in cirrhosis, a condition in which scar tissue replaces normal liver tissue, and impairs the ability of the liver to function. Chronic use can also result in permanent damage to the CNS, partly due to a poor diet regimen and diminished intake of vitamin B1 (thiamine).

Barbiturates

Barbiturates are used as sedatives, hypnotics, anesthetics, and anticonvulsants. They differ in how fast they produce effects and how long the effects last. Barbiturates are classified as ultrashort, short, intermediate, and long acting, and are in Schedules II, III, or IV.

Street names of commonly abused barbiturates describe the color and markings on the actual pill. Amytal® (amobarbital): blue heavens; Butisol® (butabarbital): bute, stoppers; Luminal® (phenobarbital): phennies and phenos; Nembutal® (pentobarbital): nembies and yellow jackets; Seconal® (secobarbital): red devils and seggies; Tuinal® (amobarbital and secobarbital): Christmas trees, rainbows, tooies. Other street names include amy's, block busters, bluebirds, downers, goofballs, pinks, and stumblers.

The Derivation of Proof

The term *proof* used for alcoholic beverages dates back to colonial days in the United States. President George Washington appointed Alexander Hamilton as his first secretary of the treasury. Hamilton levied a 10-cents/gallon tax on whiskey. The citizens of Pennsylvania—a chief source of whiskey—rebelled, but their famous "Whiskey Rebellion" was suppressed. To determine the content of alcohol in the whiskey, gunpowder was moistened with the alcohol-containing product and then ignited. If the alcohol content was high enough, the product burnt, and this was considered 100 proof. At least 50% alcohol was required for the gunpowder to burn. The government said that 100 proof, or 50% alcohol by volume, was to be the standard for American liquor. Yet, the 10-cents/gallon tax was placed on all whiskey, even if below proof. Today, the proof number is always twice the percentage number of the concentration of alcohol in the product.

Barbiturates are usually taken orally, sometimes with alcohol to increase the intoxicating effect, or by injection. The ultrashort-acting barbiturate Pentothal® produces surgical anesthesia within about one minute after intravenous administration. The onset of action of the short- and intermediate-acting barbiturates taken orally for insomnia is from 10 to 60 minutes, and the effects last up to six hours. Barbiturates distribute to body fat and are found in breast milk. They may cause drowsiness, slow heartbeat, and shortness of breath in babies of nursing mothers who are taking these drugs.

Barbiturates are metabolized in the liver via hydroxylation and glucuronide conjugation. Short-acting barbiturates are excreted in the urine as metabolites for about one to four days, while long-acting barbiturates are excreted for two to three weeks.

Barbiturates overdosing may occur readily. Since tolerance develops to the behavioral effects but not to the respiratory effects, increasing the dosage may result in death. Also, because of amnesia-causing effects, people forget that they took their medication and may proceed to take additional doses, which may lead to respiratory depression and death.

Benzodiazepines

Trade names of some benzodiazepines are Ativan® (lorazepam), Dalmane® (flurazepam), Halcion® (triazolam), Klonopin® (clonazepam), Librium® (chlordiazepoxide), Restoril® (temazepam), Serax® (oxazepam), Valium® (diazepam), Versed® (midazolam), and Xanax® (alprazolam). Some street names include benzos, downers, and goofballs. The "date rape drug" Rohypnol® (flunitrazepam) has its own group of names, including forget-me pill, Mexican valium, mind erasers, R2, roches, roofies, rope, and rophies (Figure 7.2). Except for Rohypnol®, which cannot be sold in the United States, the benzodiazepines are listed as Schedule IV drugs.

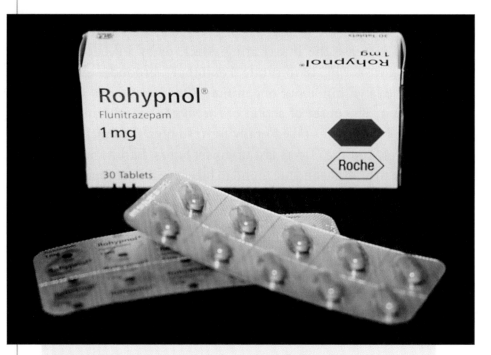

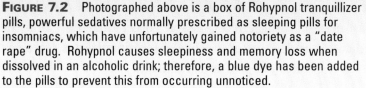

FIGURE 7.2 Photographed above is a box of Rohypnol tranquillizer pills, powerful sedatives normally prescribed as sleeping pills for insomniacs, which have unfortunately gained notoriety as a "date rape" drug. Rohypnol causes sleepiness and memory loss when dissolved in an alcoholic drink; therefore, a blue dye has been added to the pills to prevent this from occurring unnoticed.

Benzodiazepines are grouped into categories depending on how fast they take effect and how long the effects last. The short-acting benzodiazepines flurazepam, temazepam, and triazolam are used to manage insomnia, and the long-acting alprazolam, chlordiazepoxide, diazepam, lorazepam, and clonazepam are used for the treatment of generalized anxiety.

Benzodiazepines are lipid soluble and are found in breast milk. They are metabolized in the liver and excreted as glucuronide metabolites at different rates. For example, the half-life of triazolam is 2 to 5 hours, while that of diazepam varies between

20 and 100 hours, and that of an active metabolite of diazepam (desmethyldiazepam), between 36 and 200 hours. This means that diazepam metabolites may be in the bloodstream up to 200 hours after a single dose. Many of the benzodiazepines are converted to the same active metabolite. For example, diazepam, temazepam, and chlordiazepoxide are all metabolized to oxazepam.

Gamma-hydroxybutyrate

GHB, a Schedule I drug, is synthesized by mixing gamma butyrolactone (GBL; street names: blue nitro, fire water, gamma G) and sodium hydroxide. GBL is a solvent in many commercial products and is not listed as illegal. If ingested, GBL is rapidly converted in the body to GHB. Another solvent, 1,4 butanediol (BD) (street names: Sucol B, zen), is metabolized in the body to GHB. GHB is a natural metabolite of GABA.

GHB is used to treat **cataplexy**, a sudden onset of muscle weakness, in narcolepsy patients. It has been used as a hypnotic, anesthetic, and aphrodisiac, and is used to treat alcohol withdrawal. Some street names include cherry meth, eclipse, EZ lay, fantasy, G, Georgia home boy, great hormones at bedtime, grievous bodily harm, liquid ecstasy, nature's Quaalude, and poor man's heroin (Figure 7.3). According to a 2004 NIDA survey, 0.7% of eighth graders, 0.8% of tenth graders, and 2.0% of twelfth graders used GHB at least once during the preceding year. In 2002, there were 3,330 emergency room admissions related to GHB, second only among **club drugs** to the hallucinogen methylenedioxymethamphetamine (MDMA).[13]

GHB used orally is rapidly absorbed, and peak effects occur in 20 to 40 minutes. The effects last for about three hours. The half-life is approximately 20 minutes. About 5% of the dose is eliminated in urine, mostly in the first four hours. Since GHB is odorless and tasteless, it can be added to someone's drink without detection. It causes a rapid induction of deep sleep and amnesia, and is used as a date rape drug. GHB is a common drug at rave parties.

Barbiturates, benzodiazepines, and GHB affect the activity of the neurotransmitter GABA, resulting in more chloride ions entering the neuron and making it more resistant to excitation. As a consequence, the output of excitatory neurotransmitters, including norepinephrine (noradrenaline), serotonin, and dopamine, is reduced.

FIGURE 7.3 Gamma-hydroxybutyrate (GHB) is manufactured in illicit home laboratories. The chemicals above were confiscated from a GHB lab in Germany.

Other CNS Depressants

Chloral hydrate, glutethimide, and methaqualone also produce a depressant effect. Chloral hydrate is dangerous to use as an anesthetic, but it has been used to treat persons undergoing withdrawal from heroin, GHB, and alcohol. A mixture of chloral hydrate and alcohol is termed a "Mickey Finn" and has been used as a date rape drug.

Glutethimide (Doriden®) was introduced in 1954 as a substitute for barbiturates. Its street names include CB, glue, and goofballs. The combination of glutethimide and codeine is called "doors and 4s" and "pancakes and syrup." The combined euphoria resembles that of heroin, and effects can last for about eight hours.

Methaqualone was marketed by William H. Rorer, Inc., under the trade name of Quaalude, and later by the Lemmon Company as Lemmon "714" tablets. Street names include bandits, drunken monkey, ludes, magwheels, quay, 714, sopors, and wagon wheels. Methaqualone was used during the 1960s and 1970s on many college campuses, and there were many reports of overdoses and deaths. The use of methaqualone has diminished greatly since the late 1980s.

Though some differences between CNS depressant drugs do exist, as a group the effects induced are very similar. They cause a state of intoxication, with signs and symptoms of euphoria, mental confusion, loss of motor coordination, blurred vision, slurred speech, nausea, vomiting, impaired judgment, decreased attention span, and amnesia. The drugs also decrease blood pressure, heart rate, and respiration.

Tolerance and psychological and physical dependence do develop. Withdrawal effects from CNS depressants include anxiety, tremors, sweating, sleep disturbances, nausea, vomiting, and headache. Hallucinations and seizures are possible. Dosage must be reduced gradually. A condition specific to the effects of alcohol is delirium tremens. This may begin as late as 14 days after cessation of alcohol consumption. The signs and symptoms include confusion, delusions, fever, sweating, increased blood pressure, and seizures. Withdrawal effects can be treated symptomatically with benzodiazepines, antiseizure medication, and nutritional supplements.

All of the CNS depressants can pass through the placenta. Newborn babies with dependent mothers may be physically dependent themselves and have withdrawal symptoms that include tremors, irritability, hyperactivity, and feeding and breathing problems. There may be birth defects such as fetal alcohol syndrome, which consists of abnormal facial features, a small head, mental retardation, and poor coordination.

Combined use of any of the drugs in this category increases the risk of death. While a single drug may not depress respiration markedly, a combination of drugs can do so. The antidote for benzodiazepine overdose is an intravenous injection of Romazicon® (flumazenil).

FORENSIC ISSUES

In the 1970s, Marcelline Burns and Herbert Moskowitz set out to standardize field sobriety tests. They selected 10 psychophysical tests in use at that time and, along with the Los Angeles police and sheriffs departments and the California Highway Patrol, tested each for accuracy in predicting whether a person had a BAC of 0.10% or higher. Of the 10 different tests, the one-leg stand, the walk-and-turn test, and the horizontal gaze nystagmus test proved to be of value in detecting lack of sobriety.

These three tests, under the sponsorship of the National Highway Traffic Safety Administration (NHTSA), were further developed under experimental conditions and under field conditions. It was found that if one failed the one-leg-stand test, the officer would be correct 65% of the time in stating that the person's BAC was above 0.10%; if the walk-and-turn test was failed, the officer would be accurate 68% of the time; and if the horizontal gaze nystagmus test was failed, accuracy would be 77%. If both horizontal gaze nystagmus and the walk-and-turn tests were failed, accuracy increased to 81%.[14] All states have established a BAC of 0.08% as the cutoff value for determining driving while intoxicated, or DWI.

Examples of actual cases involving alcohol include DWI, motor vehicle accidents (involving alcohol in either pedestrian or driver), rape, personal injury (tripping or falling), burglary, theft, assault, and attempted murder. In many cases, it was necessary to calculate the BAC at the time of the accident or other event that had occurred hours before the breath or blood sample was taken (a process known as "back extrapolation").

In one particular case, a young man attacked a public figure with a knife. He was immediately apprehended and charged with attempted murder. At trial, testimony revealed that during the previous 24 hours, the man had consumed enormous amounts of alcohol and had used marijuana. The defense argued that this amount of alcohol plus marijuana had impaired the defendant's judgment and perception, and that he could not have been able to form the intent to kill. Testimony involved the pharmacology of both drugs, calculation of the BAC at about 0.40%, and the effect of both drugs on the defendant's mental capabilities. The jury returned a verdict of guilty of assault and weapons possession, but not attempted murder. The man was sentenced to 5 to 15 years.

In some states, lawsuits known as "dram shop" cases arise when someone injured by a driver under the influence of alcohol sues the bar or restaurant that had earlier served alcohol to the driver while the latter was visibly intoxicated. Testimony in those cases focused on the number and type of drinks served, the interval of drinking, when the last drink was served, the time of the accident, and the rate of alcohol metabolism.

The barbiturate butalbital is sold in combination with aspirin or acetaminophen (Fiorinal® or Fioricet®, respectively) for treatment of migraine and chronic tension headaches. When providing a urine sample, consumption of either of these drugs must be mentioned.

The benzodiazepine Rohypnol® has a rapid onset of action and has been used as a date rape drug. The victim will have no memory of any events that occurred while under the influence of the drug. The effects begin in about 20 to 30 minutes and peak in about two hours.

GHB can be formed from GABA and is found naturally in human tissues. In non-GHB users, however, GHB is usually not detected in blood or urine samples. Also, since GHB appears to form in blood postmortem, a finding of GHB is not indicative of use unless there is evidence of oral intake. Because of its short half-life, GHB is not found in blood 8 hours after use or in urine after 24 hours. However, lack of GHB after these intervals is not indicative that GHB was not used in an alleged rape. There are many reports of GHB being involved in overdoses, motor vehicle accidents, and deaths.

SUMMARY

CNS depressants are drugs that decrease brain activity, resulting in both behavioral and physiological changes. The effects of alcohol on coordination, speech, and cognitive functions are familiar to most people. The effects of barbiturates are similar to alcohol. In low doses, barbiturates act as sedatives: increased doses have a hypnotic or sleep-inducing effect; and still larger doses have anticonvulsant and anesthetic activity, and can lead to respiratory depression, coma, and death. Barbiturate addicts must be withdrawn from the drug gradually to avoid severe withdrawal symptoms such as convulsions. The benzodiazepines, introduced as alternatives to barbiturates to manage insomnia and anxiety, can also induce amnesia and have been used as date rape drugs. GHB, which causes an alcohol-like effect and amnesia, is found at rave parties and has been used as a date rape drug. Tolerance and psychological and physical dependence develop to CNS depressants.

Opioids

There are many different opioids, and this chapter will focus on a few that are most commonly abused. Opium is the milky latex that seeps out of cuts made into the unripe seed capsule of the poppy plant, *Papaver somniferum* (Figure 8.1). Opium contains two pharmacologic groups of chemicals: the phenanthrenes, which includes morphine, codeine, and thebaine; and the benzylisoquinolines, which includes papaverine and noscapine. The poppy plant grows in Burma, Thailand, Cambodia, Laos, India, Pakistan, Afghanistan, Turkey, Mexico, Brazil, and Colombia.

The effects of opium have been known as far back as 3,000 B.C. In 1803, the German pharmacist Frederick Sertürner isolated morphine from the poppy plant. He named the drug morphine after Morpheus, the Greek god of dreams, and, in 1832, codeine was isolated. Heroin was synthesized in 1874. Many years ago, these drugs were termed narcotics, because of their ability to produce sleep. Today, the word *narcotic* is sometimes used incorrectly to denote all drugs of abuse. The natural opium-derived drugs are more correctly termed opiates, and together with other natural (opioid-like endorphin

FIGURE 8.1 Opium is collected by slitting the seed capsule of an unripe opium poppy. A milky substance containing opium oozes out and soon hardens. The hardened substance is then scraped off and purified.

peptides present in brain tissue) and synthetic drugs that have morphine-like activity, are called opioids. Opioids are used for their analgesic (pain relief), antidiarrheal, and antitussive, or cough suppressant, effects.

There are many synthetic derivatives of morphine and codeine in use today medicinally, including hydrocodone (Hycodan® and Vicodin®), hydromorphone (Dilaudid®), and oxycodone (Percodan®, Percocet®, and OxyContin®, a controlled-release form with street names of hillbilly heroin and poor man's heroin). Other compounds that have morphine-like activity include meperidine (Demerol®), methadone (Dolophine®, synthesized in Germany during World War II because of a shortage of morphine), propoxyphene (Darvon®; street names include pink ladies and pumpkin seeds), and fentanyl (Duragesic®, also known as Apache, China white, goodfellas, murder 8, and Tango and Cash). A designer drug variation of fentanyl, called 3-methylfentanyl, is 6,000 times more potent than morphine. Dextromethorphan is an antitussive available over the counter in many products, including Coricidin HBP®, Dimetapp®, Sudafed® preparations, and Robitussin-DM®. Its street names include candy, CCC (or Triple C, for Coricidin Cough & Cold), DM, DXM, and Robo. Use of Robitussin-DM® is termed "Robo-copping" or "Robo-tripping," and use of Coricidin is termed "skittling."

Some street names for morphine are cube juice, hard stuff, hocus, M, Miss Emma, monkey, and white stuff. Names for opium includes big O, black stuff, Chinese tobacco, Dover's powder, joy plant, and zero. Street names for heroin include dope, H, horse, junk, skag, and smack. The mixture of heroin and cocaine is termed a speedball. Names for codeine include Captain Cody, Cody, and schoolboy, and it is found in combination with glutethimide.

Heroin is a Schedule I drug; morphine, codeine, fentanyl, hydrocodone, hydromorphone, and oxycodone are Schedule II drugs; codeine plus aspirin or acetaminophen is Schedule III; propoxyphene is Schedule IV; and codeine sold over the counter is Schedule V.

PHARMACOLOGY OF OPIOIDS

Depending on the type, opioids can be injected, smoked, snorted, or taken orally. Smoking heroin is termed "chasing the dragon." Controlled-release oral tablets of morphine (MS-Contin®) or of oxycodone (OxyContin®) should never be crushed or chewed, as the entire dose of opioid released at once may be toxic.

Oral opiates are absorbed well from the intestinal tract. Morphine, however, is significantly metabolized via first-pass metabolism and is excreted via enterohepatic circulation. Heroin crosses the blood-brain barrier much more efficiently than morphine, resulting in a greater effect (Figure 8.2). Opioids are distributed to many organs and are found in breast milk. They cross the placenta, and infants born to mothers who abused opioids during pregnancy show signs of dependence and withdrawal. About 10% of codeine is **demethylated** to produce morphine that is responsible for codeine's analgesic effect. The half-life of morphine, codeine, and heroin is two to four hours. Only about 10% of morphine is excreted in urine unchanged, and heroin, morphine, oxycodone, and codeine can be detected in urine for up to two days after use. Opioids act on several receptors, namely, mu (μ), believed responsible for the "high" as well as for the analgesia, sedation, and depression of respiration, kappa (κ), delta (δ), and sigma (σ).

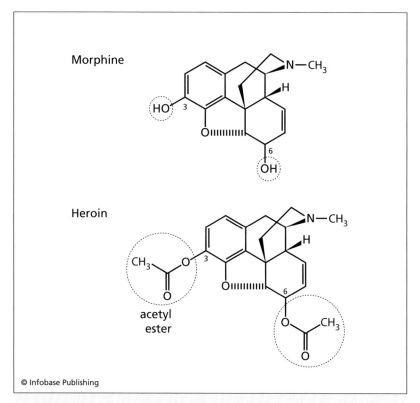

Morphine

Heroin

acetyl
ester

© Infobase Publishing

FIGURE 8.2 Heroin is a derivative of morphine. It can be manufactured synthetically by replacing the two hydroxyl (OH) groups in morphine with two acetate (CH_3COO) groups; thus, an alternate name for heroin is diacetylmorphine.

Dextrorphan, the metabolite of dextromethorphan, blocks the NMDA receptor.

Behavioral effects of opioids include euphoria, sedation and mental clouding. Physiological effects include respiratory depression, decreased heart rate, contraction of the pupil, constipation, nausea, and vomiting. Opioids can also release histamine from body stores, causing severe itching, hypotension, sweating, and flushing.

Overdosing causes stupor and coma. Pulmonary edema occurs, and froth can be seen coming from the nose and mouth. An antidote for an opioid overdose is naloxone (Narcan®), which can rapidly displace the opioid from the receptor. Overuse of dextromethorphan can induce euphoria, sedation, ataxia, increased awareness, sweating, elevated blood pressure, arrhythmia, hallucinations, and coma. Some of the dextromethorphan effects resemble those of phencyclidine.

Opioids induce tolerance, and severe withdrawal signs and symptoms occur 8 to 12 hours after the last dose. The individual begins to yawn, and the eyes begin to tear. Sweating, fever, increased blood pressure and heart rate, piloerection (goose flesh), dilated pupils, insomnia, chills, gastrointestinal and muscle cramps, nausea, vomiting, and diarrhea may last for 7 to 10 days. Thus, to abruptly stop taking opioids, known as "going cold turkey," is a very painful and stressful period for about a week.

Methadone, distributed at medical centers, is cross-tolerant with morphine and heroin and reduces the withdrawal effects. Methadone's effects are long lasting and can be given once daily, thereby reducing the time spent trying to obtain drug. The dose of methadone is gradually lowered until the individual no longer needs any opioid.

FORENSIC ISSUES

A positive urine test result for opioids does not necessarily mean that the individual used drugs illegally. The GC/MS instrument is very sensitive, and any morphine detected could have come from the individual having eaten poppy seed-containing bagels or pastries shortly before the test. Also, many people are prescribed opioid-containing analgesics such as Tylenol® with codeine, Percodan®, and Percocet®, and their urine samples will test positive. At the time of urine collection, it is important to list the foods or drugs taken in the prior 24 to 48 hours. Several quinolone antibiotics, including levofloxacin (Levaquin®) and ofloxacin (Floxin®), can give false-positive results for opioids in screening procedures.

The initial metabolism of heroin involves loss of one acetyl group, forming 6-monoacetylmorphine, or 6-MAM. If 6-MAM is detected in body fluids and tissues, it can only have come from heroin. When 6-MAM is further metabolized, it loses the second acetyl group and forms morphine. At this point, finding morphine, is not helpful in determining whether the individual had used heroin or morphine, or even codeine, since it also is metabolized to morphine.

Examples of cases involving opioids include murder, accidental death, positive urine drug test results in child custody cases, and medical malpractice. In one medical malpractice case against a physician and a pharmacist, a man who had been prescribed Tussionex® was found dead. Tussionex® contains hydrocodone and an antihistamine, chlorpheniramine, and is used to treat cough, cold, and allergy. At autopsy, blood analysis revealed the presence of high levels of hydrocodone and also the benzodiazepines flurazepam and diazepam. Urine analysis indicated the presence of unchanged cocaine, suggesting use within the last 8 to 12 hours. All the data led to the conclusion that the deceased had taken an unusually large amount of Tussionex® that by itself might have been lethal, but that the combination of hydrocodone and the nonprescribed benzodiazepines depressed the CNS and caused death.

SUMMARY

The opioids contain natural and synthetic compounds that are medicinally used as analgesic, antidiarrheal, and antitussive agents. Opioids are CNS depressants and decrease blood pressure, heart rate, and respiration. They can cross the placenta to affect the fetus. Abuse of opioids can lead to tolerance and physical dependence. Withdrawal is severe, and several drugs, based on cross-tolerance, have been used to minimize withdrawal and to wean the individual off opioids.

9

Hallucinogens

There are two subgroups of hallucinogens: the indolealkyl-amine derivatives and the phenethylamine derivatives. The indolealkylamine derivatives, which are related to the neurotransmitter serotonin (5-HT), include lysergic acid diethylamide (LSD), psilocybin, N,N-dimethyltryptamine (DMT), and bufotenine. The phenethylamine derivatives are related to the neurotransmitters epinephrine, norepinephrine, and dopamine, and include mescaline and methylenedioxymethamphetamine (MDMA, also known as ecstasy). All of the hallucinogens are Schedule I drugs.

In 1938, at the Sandoz pharmaceutical firm, a Swiss scientist, Dr. Albert Hofmann, synthesized LSD from lysergic acid, which is produced by the fungus *Claviceps purpurea* that infects rye and other grains. He took the drug himself and was amazed at the psychosis-mimicking (psychotomimetic) effects. The CIA secretly tested LSD as a mind-controlling drug, and these experiments resulted in at least one death and led to congressional and presidential investigations.[15] Some street names for LSD include acid, blotters, California sunshine, Lucy in the sky with diamonds, panes, paper, pyramids, stamps, sugar, trips, and white lightning.

Psilocybin can be found in over 100 species of mushrooms in Mexico, Central America, and northwestern and southeastern parts of the United States. Some of the common mushroom varieties are *Psilocybe mexicana, Psilocybe cubensis, Psilocybe azurescens,* and *Psilocybe cyanescen.* Street names include Alice, magic mushrooms, purple passion, shrooms, and silly putty.

DMT is found in the South American plants *Virola calophylla* and *Mimosa hostilis,* and in grasses, mushrooms, toads, grubs, and fish, and has been used by the Amazon natives for spiritual effects. DMT was synthesized in 1931.

Bufotenine was isolated from skin and parotid gland of the toad *Bufo vulgaris* in 1893, and from plants and mushrooms. It is also found in the toad *Bufo marinus* that lives in the southern part of the United States and the Caribbean, and in *Bufo alvarius,* found in the southwestern United States. Amazon explorers had described poisoning by toad and mushroom preparations more than 400 years ago. Street names include black stone, Chan Su, Chinese love stones, cohoba, rock hard, Stud 100, and toad.

Mescaline is an alkaloid isolated from the peyote cactus, species *Lophophora williamsii* or *Anhalonium lewinii,* that grows in the southwestern United States and in Mexico. Mescaline is found in "buttons" that grow on top of the plant. Aztec and Native American Indians used the buttons in religious rites and for treatment of snakebite, flu, and arthritis. Some street names include bad seed, blue caps, cactus buttons, devils root, mesc, moon, peyote, shaman, and tops.

Methylenedioxymethamphetamine (MDMA) was synthesized in 1912 and patented in 1914 by Merck as an appetite suppressant, but was never marketed (Figure 9.1). Since the middle 1980s, MDMA, which is primarily known as ecstasy, has become a popular drug at raves. The final product often contains other stimulants such as caffeine or cocaine. Users of ecstasy report enhanced communication and empathy with others. A 2002

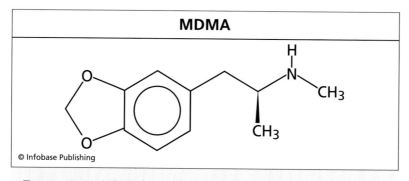

FIGURE 9.1 MDMA (3,4-methylenedioxymethamphetamine) is a synthetic drug better known by its street name, ecstasy. It has the chemical formula $C_{11}H_{15}NO_2$.

NIDA study found that 4.3% of eighth graders, 6.6% of tenth graders, and 10.5% of twelfth graders used ecstasy at least once. A 2004 study found that 1.7% of eighth graders, 2.4% of tenth graders, and 4% of twelfth graders had used ecstasy at least once in the preceding year. [16]

Street names for MDMA, besides ecstasy, include Adam, E, ecsta eve, Eve, H-bomb (with heroin), hug drug, love drug, M, pikachu (with PCP), psychedelic amphetamine, Versace, X, and XTC. Tablets of ecstasy usually have imprinted monograms. Some examples include E-mail, D&G, Rolex, Nike, Fred Flintstone, Pokemon, Batman, and cupid.

PHARMACOLOGY OF HALLUCINOGENS

LSD is the most potent psychoactive drug and is believed to be 3,000 to 4,000 times more potent than mescaline. LSD is used in tablets (microdots), capsules, sugar cubes, thin squares of gelatin (window panes), or liquid form, or it is added to absorbent paper with various designs that is cut into small squares and placed on the tongue (Figure 9.2). It is absorbed rapidly from the gastrointestinal tract, and effects begin within 5 to 10 minutes. Animal studies indicate that LSD can pass the placenta, but reports of birth defects and chromosomal changes have not been proven conclusively. The half-life of LSD is about three hours. LSD can be detected in urine after one to two hours and for about four days.

Psilocybin mushrooms are chewed or used to make a tea, or ground into powder. The effects begin approximately 30

FIGURE 9.2 Acid tabs, shown above, are impregnated with "acid," or lysergic acid diethylamide (LSD), a psychedelic drug and hallucinogen, illegal in most countries but still commonly used for recreational purposes. LSD is colorless and odorless, and its effects are unpredictable.

to 60 minutes later and last for about four hours. It is converted in the liver to psilocin, the biologically active molecule. Psilocybin and glucuronidated metabolites are detected in urine within several hours after use and for up to three days thereafter.

DMT and bufotenine are destroyed in the intestine, and thus cannot be taken orally. Instead, they are smoked or snorted. DMT can also be injected, and effects begin in two to five minutes. The effects last less than 30 minutes, and, because of its short-acting effects, DMT is known as the "businessman's lunch." Bufotenine's effects last from 4 to 12 hours.

Mescaline-containing "buttons" on top of the peyote cactus can be chewed or used to make a tea, or ground into a powder. Mescaline is absorbed rapidly, and effects begin between one-half and two hours after ingestion. Its half-life is six hours. Much of mescaline is excreted unchanged in urine as soon as one hour after use and for up to four days. In animal studies, there is evidence that mescaline passes into the fetus and can induce malformations. Mescaline, LSD, psilocybin, and DMT all activate the same serotonin receptor subtype in the brain.

Ecstasy is taken orally in pill or capsule form, and effects begin about 45 minutes later and last three to six hours (Figure 9.3). Large amounts of drug can be detected in urine as soon as one hour after use and for about three days. The half-life of ecstasy is about eight hours. Ecstasy works on serotonin-containing neurons. Initially, it leads to an increased release of serotonin from nerves and inhibits reuptake, resulting in increased serotonin levels in the synapse. Eventually, because of depletion and permanent damage to the serotonin nerve networks, it results in decreased serotonin levels. It also releases dopamine and norepinephrine. Ecstasy causes euphoria, an increase in energy, increased communication, and increased sexual drive. In addition, ecstasy causes teeth

FIGURE 9.3 Ecstasy tablets are manufactured in a variety of colors and are often imprinted with a monogram.

grinding and breakdown of skeletal muscle. Tolerance develops rapidly.

Effects of hallucinogens can be unpredictable, depending on the drug and dose, the user's expectations, and the surroundings in which the drug is used. Physiological effects common to all hallucinogens include dilated pupils; increased heart rate, blood pressure, and body temperature; sweating; nausea and vomiting; headache; loss of appetite; sleeplessness; dry mouth; shaking; speech difficulty; loss of coordination; muscle rigidity; and visual sensitivity to light. Common psychological effects include delusions and hallucinations, including the ability to see music and hear colors (an effect called synesthesia). The user's sense of time and self can change, and he or she may feel several different emotions all at once or swing rapidly from one emotion to another, and exhibit impaired concentration, judgment, and attention. Paranoia, anxiety, confusion, and depression may develop. Tolerance develops, but not signs of withdrawal. Cross-tolerance to LSD, mescaline, and psilocybin has been reported. LSD users refer to their experience as a "trip" and to adverse reactions of terrifying thoughts of insanity, despair, and death as a "bad trip." This can last for several hours. Many LSD users experience "flashbacks," recurrences of certain aspects of a person's LSD experience, without the user having taken the drug again. A flashback occurs suddenly, often without warning, and may occur within a few days

PiHKAL and TiHKAL

Alexander "Sasha" Shulgin received his Ph.D. in biochemistry from the University of California, Berkeley. His research interests are in psychiatry and pharmacology. A student aroused his interest in MDMA, and in the late 1970s and early 1980s, Shulgin introduced MDMA to psychologists for use in their patients. Shulgin synthesized and tested on himself, and on a small group of friends, hundreds of psychoactive chemicals. Shulgin and his wife Ann collected the entire chemical synthetic data and descriptions of effects, and published several books including *PiHKAL (Phenethylamines I Have Known and Loved): A Chemical Love Story* and *TiHKAL (Tryptamines I Have Known and Loved): The Continuation*.

or even years after LSD use. Dysphoric effects following use of hallucinogens include sadness, anxiety, memory impairment, and depression.

FORENSIC ISSUES

Each dose of LSD (about 0.05 mg) is too small to be sold and administered separately. A solution of LSD is applied to a carrier, such as paper, which is then cut up into individual portions. A person convicted of distributing LSD is sentenced according to the entire weight of material seized, including the carrier. Since carriers may be of different weights, the same number of doses of LSD may carry different sentences. Although recognizing the unfairness of this law, the Supreme Court ruled that the weight of LSD does include carrier and that it is up to Congress to change the statute.

In one actual case, a man used LSD and, within an hour thereafter, killed a store owner. The defendant claims that he awoke one morning and took five to six Fioricet® tablets, went out and purchased two bags of heroin, and took cocaine hourly for five hours. Then, for the first time in six years, he took six "hits" of LSD. His memory afterward was vague, until he realized that he was in police custody. He apparently entered a store, had an argument with the owner, and killed him. People witnessing the events captured and held the defendant until the police arrived. The man was found guilty of murder.

SUMMARY

There are two main chemical categories of hallucinogens: the indolealkylamine derivatives, which are related to the neurotransmitter serotonin, and the phenethylamine derivatives, which are related to norepinephrine and dopamine. Hallucinogens alter the senses affecting sight, sound, touch, taste, and smell. They induce vivid images and sounds, profound emotional episodes, altered perceptions of time and space, out-of-body experiences, and, if doses are high enough, convulsions. Tolerance does develop. There is some evidence that ecstasy can cause irreversible damage to serotonin neurons. Effects usually begin within minutes and can last for many hours. With LSD, flashbacks of prior experiences can occur without the user having taken more of the drug.

Dissociative Anesthetics

Dissociative anesthetics induce analgesia in patients who are conscious but feel removed from their surrounding environment. The two prominent dissociative anesthetics are phencyclidine (PCP) and ketamine. PCP is a synthetic drug first prepared in 1926 and tested as a general anesthetic for surgical patients in the late 1950s under the trade name of Sernyl®. Although anesthetized, patients given phencyclidine remained conscious, staring, and rigid, without depression of respiration or cardiovascular function. Following surgery, however, patients became delirious, disoriented, and unmanageable, and phencyclidine testing was discontinued. Until 1978, the drug was still used legally for veterinary anesthesia under the name Sernylan®. In the late 1960s, PCP became popular as a street drug in San Francisco and was termed the "peace pill." In spite of reports of "bad trips" and violent behavior, its popularity increased during the 1970s and 1980s. Though illicit use of PCP declined with the rise of cocaine use in the 1980s, it now appears to be increasing.

Street names for PCP include angel dust, cadillac, CJ, crystal, dust, elephant tranquilizer, embalming fluid, hog, jet fuel, juice, killer weed, love boat, Peace, PeaCePill, rocket fuel, sherms

FIGURE 10.1   Drug enforcement agents in the Phillipines surround confiscated bags and vials of ketamine after an apartment raid in May 2005. The drugs had an estimated street value of $150,000 U.S. dollars. In powdered form, ketamine has an appearance similar to cocaine but a vastly different pharmacology.

(using cigarettes produced by Nat Sherman Tobacco Company for dipping into liquid PCP), whack, and zoom. When used in combination with embalming fluid (which contains formaldehyde, methanol, and ethanol), it is known on the street as wets, illy, and fry. It is also used in combination with heroin, LSD, and marijuana. The combination with marijuana is termed killer joints, crystal supergrass, or, in Spanish, yerba mala. PCP is listed in Schedule II.

Calvin Stevens developed ketamine while working at Parke-Davis in 1961. It is used as a veterinary and human anesthetic, and is a Schedule III drug. It was widely used as a field anesthetic in the Vietnam War, and it entered the rave scene in the early 1990s. Ketamine has been used as a date rape drug. Street names include baby food, cat Valium, honey oil, jet, K, keets, ket, special K, super acid, super C, and vitamin K (Figure 10.1). Trade names are Ketalar®, Ketajet®, and Ketaset®.

PHARMACOLOGY OF PCP AND KETAMINE

Both PCP and ketamine can be used as a liquid or solid and can be injected, ingested, snorted, or smoked when sprinkled on marijuana or parsley leaves. Heat destroys much of the drug.

Peak blood levels occur within 15 minutes after smoking. The effects last for approximately 4 hours, although it may take more than 24 hours for an individual to return to a normal state. The drugs are stored in fatty tissue and released slowly. PCP has a long half-life ranging from many hours to days, and the PCP glucuronide metabolite can be found in urine for several days or weeks. PCP is found in breast milk. The half-life of ketamine is three to four hours, and metabolites of ketamine are excreted in urine. PCP and ketamine cross the placental barrier, and infants of chronic abusers have been born with cerebral palsy, facial deformities, and behavioral abnormalities.

PCP and ketamine bind to the NMDA receptor and block the neurotransmitter glutamate. PCP also blocks reuptake of dopamine, norepinephrine, and serotonin. Because so many neurotransmitters are affected, the signs and symptoms of PCP intoxication are numerous and varied.

The acute behavioral effects of PCP and ketamine include euphoria, distortion of the senses and of time, impaired judgment, anxiety, sedation, analgesia, dizziness, dissociation from surroundings, amnesia, psychosis, panic attacks, paranoia, violent behavior, hallucinations, catatonia (a condition characterized by bizarre rigid positions and unresponsiveness), coma, and seizure. People may have thoughts of death and dying, and are susceptible to suggestion and manipulation. Under the influence of PCP, individuals have shown very bizarre behavior, including lying down in traffic, suddenly murdering or raping family members, and robbing a bank using a broom. Often the individual cannot recall any of the events.

The physiological effects include an increase in blood pressure and body temperature, nystagmus, slurred speech, ataxia, blurred vision, excessive sweating and salivation, fast heart rate, nausea, vomiting, and extraordinary strength. Deaths have been recorded from heart or respiratory failure.

Tolerance to dissociative anesthetics does develop. Psychological dependence is greater than physical dependence, although withdrawal symptoms may last for several weeks and include diarrhea, chills, tremor, anxiety, depression, and irritability. Prolonged use of PCP may induce permanent learning disabilities, amnesia, depression, and antisocial behavior.

FORENSIC ISSUES

Examples of actual cases involving PCP include driving while impaired, murder, kidnapping, robbery, rape, and burglary. In one particular case, a young woman driver struck another car, and the two occupants were killed. The driver was apprehended

Drug Effects: Animals Versus Humans

All medication needs to be approved by the Food and Drug Administration (FDA) before it can be released to the public in the United States. Many of the pharmacology studies of a drug's efficacy and safety are first done on laboratory animals. This is because there is much similarity in the anatomy, physiology, and biochemistry of animals and humans, and there is much experimental evidence showing similarity in response to many different drugs. Arguments in a lawsuit that a specific chemical is causally linked to an individual's injury or behavior often use data from animal studies.

However, occasionally there are responses in humans that are unexpected based upon results from animal studies. The response to dissociative anesthetics is a good example of one such difference. Whereas humans exhibit delirium following treatment with PCP, animals exhibit sedation. Different metabolic pathways or rates of metabolism, and differences in mode of elimination between animals and humans, might account for the variation in responses. For example, rats do not have a gall bladder and dogs sweat minimally. It is easy to see that choosing the wrong species in animal tests could result in inaccurate data relevant to humans. Nevertheless, preclinical testing is necessary, and there is much research today to develop **in vitro** in the laboratory) procedures that can predict human **in vivo** (in the body) responses. As more of these tests prove to be reliable, fewer animals will be used in research.

five hours later, and a blood test revealed a significant amount of PCP. She admitted to smoking PCP about 20 minutes before the accident. Testimony for the prosecution at both a grand jury hearing and at the subsequent trial explained PCP pharmacokinetics and the effects of PCP on mental functions and coordination. The defendant was found guilty of vehicular manslaughter and sentenced to two to six years.

SUMMARY

PCP and ketamine are dissociative anesthetics. They can induce analgesia without loss of consciousness. The individual appears awake but will not remember the experience, and vital signs such as respiration and heart rate are not impaired. The drugs distort perceptions of sight and sound, and produce feelings of detachment and dissociation from the environment and self. Persons abusing PCP exhibit very bizarre behavior and may become violent.

Inhalants

11

Inhalants of abuse are substances whose volatile vapors can be inhaled either through the nose or the mouth into the lungs and then travel to the brain, where they induce euphoria and mind-altering effects. In the late 1700s, an English chemist, Joseph Priestley, discovered that nitrous oxide gas has mind-altering and anesthetic effects, and, in the 1830s, chloroform was discovered to have anesthetic effects as well. Many of the volatile solvents, paint thinners, gasoline degreasers, and glues were abused during World War I and subsequently, but it was not until 1959 that inhalant abuse was first documented in the media, in Denver, Colorado, and then use spread to other cities. Inhalants are common among adolescents and are often the first drugs of abuse because they are inexpensive, difficult to detect, and easily available. During 2004, 9.6% of 8th graders, 5.9% of 10th graders, and 4.2% of 12th graders had used inhalants.[17]

Inhalants are found in many commercial products and are not listed as controlled substances. They can be solvents such as toluene, found in paint thinner, degreaser, nail polish remover, gasoline, and glue; propellants such as butane and propane,

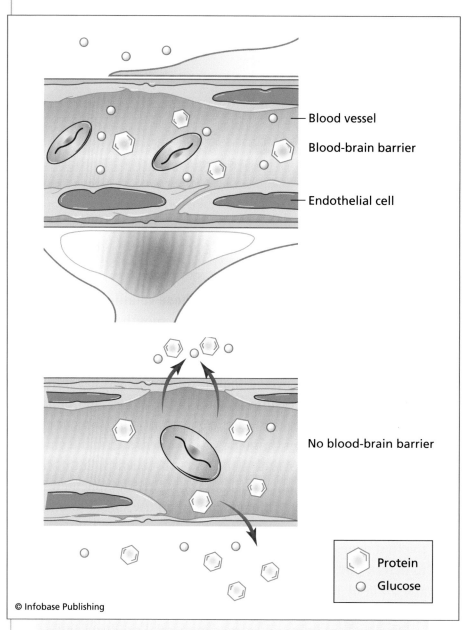

Blood vessel

Blood-brain barrier

Endothelial cell

No blood-brain barrier

Protein

Glucose

© Infobase Publishing

Figure 11.1 The blood-brain barrier prevents the passage of large molecules, such as proteins, into the brain. Small molecules, such as glucose and molecules found in drugs of abuse, are able to pass through the barrier.

used in hair sprays and cooking sprays; gases, including medical anesthetics such as chloroform and nitrous oxide (laughing gas, also used as propellant for whipped cream and inhaled from balloons); and nitrites, including amyl nitrite and isobutyl nitrite. Many of the inhalants are flammable, and people who use them can suffer serious burns.

Some street names for inhalants include air blast, hippie crack, moon gas, poor man's pot, rush, and snappers. Amyl nitrite is known as amies, pearls, and poppers. Nitrous oxide is known as hysteria, laughing gas, NOZ, shoot the breeze, and whippets.

PHARMACOLOGY OF INHALANTS

Vapors can be inhaled directly from a can, a bag (called "bagging"), a balloon, or an inhalant-soaked cloth (called "huffing"). Inhalants enter the bloodstream through the capillaries on lung alveoli and, being highly lipid soluble, easily pass the blood-brain barrier (Figure 11.1). They interfere with ion movement in the cell membrane at the glutamate or GABA receptor, resulting in an inhibition of transmission.

Depending on the dose, inhalants can cause effects ranging from intoxication to anesthesia. Intoxication can last only a few minutes or several hours, if inhalants are taken repeatedly. Initially, users may feel slightly stimulated, euphoric, and light-headed. With repeated inhalations, users may feel less inhibited and less in control, and can hallucinate. Other effects include headache, muscle weakness, abdominal pain, severe mood swings and violent behavior, numbness and tingling of the hands and feet, nausea, and lack of coordination. Inhaling highly concentrated amounts of chemicals can quickly lead to arrhythmia, heart failure, and death. This is known as "sudden sniffing death." The nitrites relax smooth muscle causing vasodilation and induce flushing, warmth, hypotension, and dizziness. For example, amyl nitrite is used as a medication to relieve angina (chest pain caused by lack of blood flow and oxygen to the heart) by dilating the coronary vessels.

Signs of inhalant abuse are unusual breath odor or chemical odor on clothing; paint or stain marks on the face, fingers, or clothing; spots or sores around the mouth; and red or runny eyes or nose. Other clues include hidden rags or clothing, or empty containers.

Chronic abuse of inhalants can cause severe, irreversible effects on the brain, heart, liver, lungs, kidneys, and blood, and can result in hearing loss, limb spasms, cognitive impairment, and various psychological and social problems. Inhalants damage the peripheral nerves, leading to muscle weakness and paralysis, and damage the nerve fibers in the CNS. Inhalant abuse during pregnancy can cause spontaneous abortion, premature delivery, and fetal abnormalities such as low birth weight, small head size, facial abnormalities, and muscle tone abnormalities similar to those occurring in fetal alcohol syndrome.

Nitrous oxide can react with vitamin B12, preventing its use in red blood cell development and resulting in anemia. Use of nitrites can rapidly result in fatal methemoglobinemia, a condition that reduces the ability of the blood to transport oxygen. In 1944, 11 men were admitted to a New York hospital with bluish discoloration of the skin due to methemoglobinemia. The city toxicologist and the health department eventually determined that salt shakers in a food establishment visited by all of the men contained sodium nitrite instead of table salt, sodium chloride.

Tolerance to inhalants can develop with frequent use, and withdrawal symptoms include sleep disturbance, irritability, jitteriness, sweating, nausea and vomiting, fast heart rate, and hallucinations or delusions. Withdrawal can last one month or longer, and the relapse rate is high.

FORENSIC ISSUES

In 1962, California enacted the first known law against glue sniffing. By 1968, 13 states and 29 counties passed anti-glue sniffing legislation prohibiting the inhalation or drinking of products such as glue or adhesive cement for the purpose of becoming intoxicated or otherwise altering mental functions.

Although not regulated under the Controlled Substances Act (CSA), many state legislatures have attempted to deter youth from buying legal products containing inhalants. As reported by the National Conference of State Legislatures, by the year 2000, 38 states had adopted laws preventing the sale and/or distribution to minors of various products commonly abused as inhalants, with penalties of fines or incarceration for offenders.

In one particular case, a man was stopped for driving while intoxicated (DWI). A breathalyzer test revealed a blood alcohol concentration (BAC) of 0.20%. The driver claimed that he had consumed only three beers within a four-hour period and that the BAC reading was incorrect. He also claimed that he had been working all day with furniture refinishing products containing volatile chemicals such as toluene, xylene, acetone, and hexane, and that these chemicals interfered with the breath test. Testimony dealt with the effects of these inhalants on behavior and coordination, and how they may have contributed to the defendant's erratic driving. However, these inhalants do not alter a breathalyzer test, and thus the jury was convinced that the 0.20% reading indicated that the defendant was lying about the number of drinks he had consumed. The driver was found guilty of DWI.

SUMMARY

Inhalants are volatile substances that produce mind-altering effects ranging from euphoria to hallucinations. Effects on brain, heart, liver, and kidneys are associated with inhalant use, including sudden sniffing death, which can occur within minutes of using highly concentrated amounts of an inhalant. Tolerance to inhalants can develop with frequent use, and, although withdrawal is possible, it occurs infrequently.

Anabolic-Androgenic Steroids

12

Anabolic-androgenic steroids (AAS) used as drugs of abuse include the natural hormone testosterone and its synthetic derivatives. Not included in this class of drugs are the female steroid hormones, estrogen, and progesterone, and the corticosteroids, such as cortisone and prednisone. More than 150 years ago, it was discovered that testes played a role in maintaining male characteristics. Testosterone, isolated from bull testes, was identified as the active chemical. It soon became evident that testosterone not only controlled masculinizing (**androgenic**) properties but could also induce muscle-building (**anabolic**) effects. Since synthetic derivatives of testosterone induce both anabolic and androgenic effects, this class of drugs is called anabolic-androgenic steroids.

Recently, two books have drawn attention to the use of steroids by baseball players, and Congress has held hearings on the extent of steroid use in this sport. The current rules provide for a 50-game suspension for a first-time steroid user, a 100-game suspension for a second-time offender, and a lifetime ban from baseball if tested positive for a third time. A NIDA survey taken in 2002 indicates that 2.5% of 8th graders, 3.5% of 10th graders, and 4.0% of 12th graders have used anabolic-androgenic steroids at least once.[18]

AAS are Schedule III drugs and are referred to as roids and juice. Products include Anadrol® (oxymetholone), Oxandrin® (oxandrolone), Dianabol® (methandrostenolone, D-bol, D-ball), Winstrol® (stanozolol), Durabolin® (nandrolone), Depo®-testosterone (testosterone, Depo-T), and Equipoise® (boldenone).

PHARMACOLOGY OF STEROIDS

Depending on the AAS, a steroid can be administered either orally or by injection (Figure 12.1). Testosterone is inactivated

Laws, Politics, and Steroids

The Anabolic Steroid Control Act of 2004 adds steroid precursor chemicals to the list of controlled substances under the Controlled Substance Act (CSA). One of the AAS that is not included on the controlled substance list is dehydroepiandrosterone (DHEA). DHEA is metabolized into testosterone in the body. This chemical, exempt under federal law, is sold in nutrition shops. Senator Orrin G. Hatch of Utah, where many dietary substance companies exist, managed to convince enough members of Congress to exclude this chemical from the list of controlled substances. Although DHEA is available to the general public, it is unlikely that sports figures will use it, as it is banned by the International Olympic Committee, the World Anti-Doping Agency, the National Collegiate Athletic Association, the National Football League, the National Basketball Association, and minor league baseball.

in the liver and has little effect if taken orally. Synthetic compounds, which are less readily metabolized, can be given by mouth, but are usually given in oil by intramuscular injection and are absorbed slowly. AAS can be detected in urine within four to six hours after use and, depending on the AAS, for weeks or months thereafter.

Unlike most drugs discussed in prior chapters, use of AAS does not result in euphoria. People use these agents for long periods of time to improve their physical appearance and athletic performance. A metabolite of testosterone, dihydrotestosterone, acts in the cell nucleus to synthesize RNA and protein molecules that result in more efficient use of nitrogen to build muscle tissue. Individuals using AAS, however, are in danger of developing a physical and psychological dependence. Withdrawal results in depressive mood, fatigue, restlessness, anorexia, insomnia, decreased libido, musculoskeletal pain, and suicidal tendencies.

Adverse reactions that can occur while taking AAS include liver toxicity, suicide, delirium, aggression (called "roid rage"), mood swings, psychosis, premature baldness, and acne. Steroids can interfere with endocrine function. For males, there is the possibility of benign prostatic hypertrophy, testicular atrophy, sterility, enlargement of breast tissue, and closure of the bone epiphysis, resulting in shortened growth. For females, the concerns include shrinking of breast size, clitoral hypertrophy, hirsutism (facial and body hair), and deepened voice. AAS have been used medically to treat osteoporosis, anemia, breast cancer, and other diseases.

FORENSIC ISSUES

In one particular case, a man attacked another with a bat. The man who was attacked took the bat and used it to hit the attacker, who later died. At the murder trial, the defense

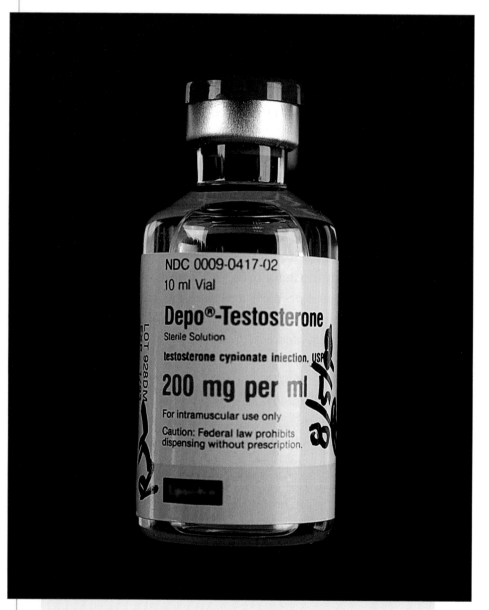

FIGURE 12.1 Anabolic-androgenic steroids, such as Depo®-Testosterone, are often injected directly into muscle tissue. In teens, steroid use can slow or halt bone growth and damage the heart, kidneys, and liver.

wanted to introduce evidence that the deceased used large amounts of AAS, and autopsy results showed that the deceased had an enlarged heart consistent with his steroid use. Such use of AAS by the attacker would have made for a strong argument that rage played a role and that the defendant had no choice but to defend himself. The defense, however, was barred because of legal technicalities from introducing this evidence and testimony. Without the evidence of AAS use, the defendant was found guilty of manslaughter.

SUMMARY

Anabolic-androgenic steroids (AAS), which are analogs of the male hormone testosterone, are used among athletes and bodybuilders. AAS alter the hormonal systems of males and females, and induce many adverse effects. In addition to the sex-related changes, violent behavior and psychological dependence can also occur. The use of AAS in professional sports as well as in high school sports has aroused considerable attention.

13

The Future of Forensic Pharmacology

In the first chapters of this book, we discussed the fields of pharmacology and toxicology, how these sciences are applied to the legal system, the role of the forensic scientist, and some of the analytical tools used to detect the presence of chemicals in bodily fluids and tissues. Drugs of abuse were chosen to illustrate practical applications of forensic pharmacology, since these drugs are often involved in legal matters. In order to establish a causal link between exposure to a chemical and an eventual outcome, the forensic scientist must understand the pharmacokinetics, pharmacodynamics, and effects of each chemical under study. Only then can one draw an accurate conclusion as to causality. Each of the eight drug chapters provided actual cases to illustrate how such information played a role in the resolution of the case. It is now of interest to look ahead and envision the role of forensic pharmacology in the future.

New chemicals are synthesized constantly. Also, many pharmacologically active chemicals continue to be found in plant life and sea life, and it can be expected that these resources will continue to provide new material. Some of the newly discovered chemicals will have antianxiety properties or be used to treat pain, and such drugs, acting in the central nervous system (CNS), may lead to drug abuse. In addition to new chemicals, people are constantly modifying existing drugs of abuse and synthesizing new drugs for recreational purposes. Consequently, either to maintain the habit of taking these drugs or because of their effects on behavior, coordination, and judgment, users may engage in criminal activity or cause injury to themselves or others. The forensic scientist needs to be knowledgeable of new legal and illegal drugs and of their pharmacological and toxicological effects.

Pharmacokinetic and pharmacodynamic studies lead to a greater understanding of chemical interactions at the molecular level and may identify specific receptors for drug activity. With more specific knowledge of how a drug works, it may become easier to more accurately establish what effects are actually caused by a particular drug. Thus, studies in these two areas of pharmacology will always be necessary.

As discussed earlier, forensic pharmacology and toxicology are not limited to the study of drugs of abuse or poisons. These fields of science also have a growing role in the legal system to help resolve civil issues related to chemical exposure and cancer causation, medical malpractice as a result of drug interactions, and product liability issues.

CHALLENGES FOR THE FUTURE

To identify the presence of new drugs, forensic scientists will always need to develop new analytical techniques. In addition, analytical techniques with greater specificity and sensitivity will continue to be developed for existing drugs.

Reporting false-positive results may send an innocent person to prison, so everything possible must be done to avoid such an outcome. Assays with enhanced sensitivity to detect both parent compound and metabolites will allow for detection of drugs over longer periods of time and for more accurate determination of when an individual was first exposed to a chemical.

Today, everyone is aware of terrorist activity. A well-known terrorist attack involving chemicals occurred in 1995 with the release of the nerve gas sarin in the subway systems of Tokyo, resulting in the death of 12 people and injury of many more. Should chemicals again be used for terrorist activity, forensic pharmacologists and toxicologists may be called upon to analyze bodily samples in order to identify the chemical, determine its mechanism of action, and propose antidotes and preventive measures.

Forensic science is an exciting and rewarding field of work. A forensic scientist is at times a scientific detective and at times a teacher, instructing the judge, attorney, and jury, and helping to promote justice. Enrollment in forensic science programs will continue to increase as new programs are established at colleges and forensic science courses are introduced at the high school level. As more industries, sports organizations, and agencies involved with supervision of children monitor their personnel for drug abuse, additional forensic scientists and laboratory facilities will be needed.

To assure that the best technology is available and that personnel are qualified, forensic science laboratories should undergo accreditation processes with periodic proficiency testing. This will assure some uniformity in procedure among different laboratories, and provide assurance that samples are analyzed correctly and data are interpreted accurately.

Thus, much work lies ahead. As the field of forensic science advances, forensic pharmacologists and toxicologists will continue to be integral players in bringing truth to our system of justice.

Solve the Cases!

The following hypothetical scenarios are intended to test your knowledge of the pharmacology of drugs of abuse and of the procedures used to resolve cases. The answers are provided at the end of the chapter.

CASE A. IMPAIRED DRIVING?

A police officer stops a car that is driving fast and erratically on a major highway. The driver stumbles slightly when stepping out of the car. The officer, a trained drug recognition expert (DRE), notices that the driver's eyes are bloodshot and the pupils are dilated. The officer sees an empty beer bottle but does not detect any unusual odor or see any signs of drugs. The DRE performs a roadside breath test, which reveals a BAC of 0.02%, and field sobriety tests, which the driver fails.

What do you suspect caused the erratic driving, and what additional tests would you suggest be performed?

CASE B. TEAM RIVALRY?

Before a big football game, the coach of Team A called in the squad for a pep talk and breakfast of juice, bagels, and donuts. As the teams took the field, the two opposing quarterbacks wished each other good luck with a Gatorade toast. Fifteen minutes into the game, the Team A quarterback began acting aggressive, anxious, and hyperactive, and then passed out. Doctors rushed onto the field and found the quarterback had slightly elevated blood pressure, heart rate, and respiration, and was sweating and salivating. The quarterback was revived, but stared into space and was nonresponsive. In the locker room, suspecting an overdose of drugs, a urine sample was collected. The results were positive for morphine and one other drug.

How do you explain the presence of morphine? Does the presence of morphine agree with the signs and symptoms exhibited by the quarterback? What other drug do you suspect was found?

CASE C. GOT AWAY WITH IT?

Following a motor vehicle accident, the driver accused of causing the accident was taken to a hospital, where a urine sample was obtained. A screening test revealed the presence of benzodiazepines. At trial, the defense expert testified that the presence of benzodiazepines in urine is not indicative of impairment. The drug might have been consumed several days prior to the accident. The jury found the defendant not guilty.

What tests would you have done at the time of the accident to help establish that the defendant was driving while impaired?

Answer to Case A: Bloodshot eyes and poor coordination are hallmark signs of marijuana intoxication. The driver may have finished smoking marijuana before getting into the car, explaining the absence of odor, or may have ingested the marijuana. The level of alcohol is too low to account for poor coordination and the failing of the field sobriety tests. A urine sample should be collected and tested by EMIT and, if positive for cannabinoids, confirmed by GC/MS.

Answer to Case B: *The finding of morphine is likely due to poppy seed bagels eaten at breakfast, but the level of morphine would be too low to exert any effects. Also, slightly elevated vital signs are not consistent with morphine's effects. The quarterback's unusual behavior before passing out and the nonresponsive stare are typical signs of PCP intoxication. Someone may have slipped the drug into Team A quarterback's Gatorade just before the good-luck toast.*

Answer to Case C: *Two types of analysis would have been helpful. An analysis of blood would have been a better indicator of causality than a urine sample. If benzodiazepines were found in the blood, the type of benzodiazepine and its concentration would have helped establish whether or not the driver was impaired. An examination by a DRE might have revealed any drug-related physiological effects, and performance of field sobriety tests might have indicated impairment.*

NOTES

1. Dietrich Milles, "History of Toxicology," Chapter 1 in *Toxicology*, 11–23.

2. Gary W. Kunsman, "Human Performance Toxicology," Chapter 2 in *Principles of Forensic Toxicology*, 13–30; and David Sandler, "Expert and Opinion Testimony," Chapter 16 in *Medical-Legal Aspects of Drugs*, 399–437.

3. *Schedules of Controlled Substances*, 21USC812.

4. L.D. Johnston, P.M. O'Malley, and J.G. Bachman, "Trends in Annual Prevalence of an Illicit Drug Use Index Among 8th, 10th and 12th graders." http://www.monitoringthefuture.org/data/04data/fig04_1.pdf.

5. Office of National Drug Control Policy, "Juveniles and Drugs." http://www.whitehousedrugpolicy.gov/drugfact/juveniles/index.html.

6. Office of Applied Studies, "Drug Abuse Warning Network, 2003: Interim National Estimates of Drug-Related Emergency Department Visits." http://www.oas.samhsa.gov/dawn/2K3interimED.pdf.

7. Substance Abuse and Mental Health Data Archive, "Overall Teen Drug Use Continues Gradual Decline; But Use of Inhalants Rises." http://www.monitoringthefuture.org.

8. Associated Press, "Health: Teenager Prescription Drug Use." http://kyw.com/siteSearch/local_story_111162950.html/resources_storyPrintableView.

9. MADD, "Fatalities and Alcohol-Related Fatalities." http://www.madd.org/stats/0,1056,9659_print,00.html.

10. NIDA, "NIDA Infofacts: Drugged Driving." http://www.nida.nih.gov/Infofacts/driving.html.

11. Office of National Drug Control Policy, "Juveniles and Drugs." http://www.whitehousedrugpolicy.gov/drugfact/juveniles/index.html.

12. California NORML, *CaNORML*, National Organization for the Reform of Marijuana Laws. http://www.canorml.org.

13. NIDA, "GHB." http://www.nida.nih.gov/infofacts/rohypnolghb.html.

14. Gary W. Kunsman, "Human Performance Toxicology," Chapter 2 in *Principles of Forensic Toxicology*, 13–30.

15. Advisory Committee on Human Radiation Experiments, Part I, Chapter 3, "Supreme Court Dissents Invoke the Nuremberg Code." http://www.eh.doe.gov/ohre/roadmap/achre/Chap3_4.html.

16. Eric Chudler, "Ecstasy-MDMA." http://faculty.washington.edu/chudler/mdma.html; and NIDA, "Ecstasy." http://teens.drugabuse.gov/facts/facts_xtc1.asp.

17. NIDA, "Inhalants." http://www.nida.nih.gov/ResearchReports/Inhalants/Inhalants2.html.

18. NIDA for Teens: Facts on Drugs, "Anabolic-Androgenic Steroids." http://teens.drugabuse.gov/facts/facts_ster1.asp.

GLOSSARY

Adulterant A substance with pharmacological effect added to or substituted for another active drug.

Alveoli Terminal air cell of the lungs where gases are exchanged.

Anabolic A steroid hormone resembling testosterone, which stimulates the growth of muscle tissue.

Analog A drug whose structure is similar to that of another drug.

Androgenic A substance causing masculinization.

Antibody A substance produced by the immune system that recognizes and neutralizes foreign substances in the body.

Antigen A substance that stimulates the production of antibodies and binds to antibodies.

Ataxia Lack of coordination of voluntary muscles; unsteady balance.

Blood-brain barrier Anatomic barrier preventing entry of certain substances from blood into the CNS.

Cataplexy A sudden muscle weakness and loss of tone that can prevent narcoleptics from achieving a normal sleep cycle.

Central nervous system (CNS) Consists of the brain and spinal cord.

Chain-of-custody To prevent specimen tampering, documentation of each step from the point of collection to the reporting of the results.

Club drugs Drugs used at rave sites.

CNS See Central nervous system.

Cross-tolerance Tolerance to a pharmacologically similar drug; one drug may be substituted for another.

Defendant A person against whom an action is brought.

Demethylated The removal of a methyl (CH_3) group.

Designer drug Any drug that is created to be chemically and pharmacologically similar to one listed in Schedules I to V and regulated under the CSA.

Diffusion The movement of a substance from an area of high concentration to an area of low concentration.

Diluent   An agent without pharmacological effect used to dilute an active drug.

Dissociative anesthetic   A drug that produces significant analgesia while the patient remains awake and feels removed from the surrounding environment, without depressing vital signs.

Drug   A chemical that affects biochemical and physiological processes of tissues or organs and is sometimes used interchangeably with the word *chemical*.

Dysphoria   A mood of general dissatisfaction, restlessness, anxiety, discomfort, and unhappiness.

Endoplasmic reticulum   A network of connecting tubules inside the cell.

Euphoria   An exaggerated feeling of well-being; mild elation.

Exhume   To remove a body from a grave.

Expert witness   An individual that a judge qualifies to offer an opinion based on knowledge, skill, experience, training, and education, if the testimony is relevant and reliable.

Forensic science   The application of science to legal issues.

Glucuronide   A water-soluble substance produced by linking glucuronic acid to another substance.

Half-life   The time required by metabolism or elimination to reduce the concentration of a chemical by 50%.

Hallucinogen   A chemical that alters sight, sound, smell, taste, and touch senses, and disturbs perception, thought, and mood.

In vitro   In glassware, tests with isolated tissue or with cell preparations.

In vivo   In the living body.

Lipophilic   Lipid loving; affinity to dissolve in fat.

Metabolite   A product of metabolism.

Monoamine oxidase inhibitor (MAOI)   A drug that inhibits the enzyme monoamine oxidase (MAO), thereby increasing the level of neurotransmitters and drugs metabolized by MAO.

Nystagmus Involuntary rotatory, horizontal, or vertical movements of the eyes most noticeable when gazing at rapidly moving objects or at fixed objects in the peripheral field of view.

Pathology Study of the structural and functional changes in the body caused by disease.

pH Hydrogen ion concentration. It is a measure of the acidity or alkalinity of a solution.

Pharmacodynamics The study of a drug's mechanisms of action on living organisms to bring about physiological and pathological changes.

Pharmacokinetics The study of a drug's absorption, distribution, metabolism, and excretion.

Pharmacologist An individual who by training and experience is a specialist in pharmacology.

Pharmacology The study of a chemical's pharmacokinetics and pharmacodynamics, and its therapeutic and toxic effects.

Physical dependence A state in which tolerance develops to a drug's effects and withdrawal symptoms appear in the absence of drug.

Plaintiff The complaining party in an action at law.

Plasma Liquid part of the blood after removing the red cells, white cells and platelets.

Postmortem redistribution After death, drugs that were concentrated in heart and adjacent organs may leak back out into the blood, producing abnormally high values.

Psychological dependence Loss of control regarding drug use either for its positive effects or in order to avoid negative effects when the drug is unavailable.

Psychosis A severe loss of contact with reality evidenced by delusions, hallucinations, disorganized speech patterns, and bizarre or catatonic behaviors.

Psychotomimetic Relating to or producing a state resembling psychosis.

Rave A party held at a licensed or unlicensed site (warehouses, fields), with loud, rhythmic techno, jungle, or zen music and laser lighting, and which may include the presence of drugs.

Recreational drug   A drug not used for medicinal purposes but for inducing euphoria and avoiding problems.

Schizophrenia   A mental disorder manifested by delusions, hallucinations, and disorganized speech and behavior.

Sensitivity   The smallest amount of the target molecule that a test can detect.

Serum   Liquid part of the blood remaining after clotting.

Specificity   Ability of a test to distinguish between highly similar target molecules.

Tolerance   The necessity of taking increasing amounts of a substance to reach desired effects.

Toxicologist   One who practices toxicology.

Toxicology   The study of a chemical's pharmacokinetics and pharmacodynamics, and its adverse or toxic effects.

Vitreous humor   Fluid inside the eyeball useful for forensic studies because it is not readily contaminated, and the concentration of drug is relatively stable.

Xenobiotic   A chemical that is strange or foreign to the body.

BIBLIOGRAPHY

Advisory Committee on Human Radiation Experiments. "Supreme Court Dissents Invoke the Nuremberg Code: CIA and DOD Human Subjects Research Scandals." ACHRE Final Report. Part I. Chap. 3. 1995. http://www.eh.doe.gov/ohre/roadmap/achre/Chap3_4.html.

Arseneault, Louise, Mary Cannon, Richie Poulton, Robin Murray, Avshalom Caspi, and Terrie E. Moffitt. "Cannabis Use in Adolescence and Risk for Adult Psychosis: Longitudinal Prospective Study." *BMJ* 325 (2002): 1212–1213.

Baden, Lindsey R., George M. Horowitz, H. Jacoby, and George M. Eliopoulos. "Quinolones and False-Positive Urine Screening for Opiates by Immunoassay Technology." *JAMA* 286 (2001): 3115–3119.

Baselt, Randall C. *Disposition of Toxic Drugs and Chemicals in Man,* 7th ed. Foster City, CA: Biomedical Publishers, 2004.

Bosy, T.Z., and K.A. Cole. "Consumption and Quantitation of delta-9-Tetrahydrocannabinol in Commercially Available Hemp Seed Oil Products." *Journal of Analytical Toxicology* 24 (2000): 562–566.

Bryson, Peter D. *Comprehensive Review in Toxicology*, 2nd ed. Rockville, MD: Aspen Publishers, Inc., 1989.

Burns, Marcelline, ed. *Medical-Legal Aspects of Drugs.* Tucson, AZ: Lawyers and Judges Publishing Company, Inc. 2003.

Cable News Network. *Education. Not Like on TV*. Time Warner Company. http://www.cnn.com/2005/EDUCATION/05/09/csi.reality.check.ap/index.html.

California NORML, *CaNORML*. National Organization for the Reform of Marijuana Laws (California Chapter). http://www.canorml.org.

Canseco, Jose. *Juiced*. New York: HarperCollins, 2005.

Center for Alternatives to Animal Testing (CAAT). Johns Hopkins University. http://caat.jhsph.edu.

Chudler, Eric. "Neuroscience for Kids." University of Washington. http://staff.washington.edu/chudler/introb.html#drug.

Congressional Findings and Declarations: Controlled Substances. U.S. Code. Title 21, Section 801.

De Forest, Peter R., R.E. Gaensslen, and Henry C. Lee. *Forensic Science: An Introduction to Criminalistics.* New York: McGraw-Hill, 1983.

Drug Policy Information Clearinghouse. "Street Terms: Drugs and the Drug Trade." Office of National Drug Control Policy. http://www. whitehousedrugpolicy.gov/pdf/street_terms.pdf.

Drunk Driving Defense. http://www.drunkdrivingdefense.com/general/ illegal-drugs.htm.

Ellenhorn, Matthew J., and Donald G. Barceloux. *Medical Toxicology: Diagnosis and Treatment of Human Poisoning.* New York: Elsevier, 1988.

Fainaru-Wada, Mark, and Lance Williams. *Game of Shadows.* New York: Penguin Group (USA) Inc., 2006.

Gahlinger, Paul M. *Illegal Drugs: A Complete Guide to Their History, Chemistry, Use, and Abuse.* New York: Plume, 2004.

Garriott, James C., ed. *Medicolegal Aspects of Alcohol,* 3rd ed. Tucson, AZ: Lawyers and Judges Publishing Company, Inc., 1996.

Gross, Jane. "In Latest Science Classes, Dead Men Do Tell Tales." *New York Times,* December 3, 2002, 1.

Hansen, Mark. "The Uncertain Science of Evidence." *ABA Journal* (July 2005): 48.

Hardman, Joel G., Lee E. Limbird, Perry B. Molinoff, Raymond W. Ruddon, and Alfred Goodman Gilman, eds. *Goodman & Gilman's The Pharmacological Basis of Therapeutics,* 9th ed. New York: McGraw-Hill, 1996.

"Health: Teenager Prescription Drug Use." *The Associated Press,* June 12, 2005. http://kyw.com/siteSearch/local_story_111162950.html/resources_ storyPrintableView.

Henderson, Yandell. "The High Proof of Liquor as a Factor in the Production of Alcoholism." *Quarterly Journal of Studies on Alcohol* 1 (1940): 1–12.

Johnston, L.D., P.M. O'Malley, and J.G. Bachman. "Trends in Annual Prevalence of an Illicit Drug Use Index Among 8th, 10th and 12th Graders." In *Monitoring the Future Study: National Results on Adolescent Drug Use. Overview of Key Findings, 2000.* Washington, DC: U.S. Department of Health and Human Services, 2001. http://www. monitoringthefuture.org/data/04data/fig04_1.pdf.

Bibliography

Kaiser, Jocelyn. "Gender in the Pharmacy: Does It Matter?" *Science* 308 (2005): 1572–1574.

Karch, Steven B., ed. *Drug Abuse Handbook.* Boca Raton, FL: CRC Press, 1998.

Karch, Steven, B. *Karch's Pathology of Drug Abuse.* 3rd ed. Boca Raton, FL: CRC Press, 2002.

Kornblut, Anne E., and Duff Wilson. "How One Pill Escaped Place on Steroid List." *New York Times,* April 17, 2005, 1.

Kunsman, Gary W. "Human Performance Toxicology." Chapter 2 in *Principles of Forensic Toxicology,* edited by Barry Levine. Washington, DC: American Association for Clinical Chemistry, Inc., 1999.

Laing, Richard R., ed. *Hallucinogens: A Forensic Drug Handbook.* London: Academic Press, 2003.

Levine, Barry, ed. *Principles of Forensic Toxicology.* Washington, DC: American Association for Clinical Chemistry, Inc., 1999.

Lobo, Ingrid A. *Inhalants (Drugs: The Straight Facts).* Philadelphia: Chelsea House Publishers, 2004.

MADD. "Fatalities and Alcohol-Related Fatalities Among 15–20 Year Olds, 2003 v. 2002." http://www.madd.org/stats/0,1056,9659_print,00.html.

Marquardt, Hans, Siegfried G. Schäfer, Roger O. McClellan, and Frank Welsch, eds. *Toxicology.* San Diego, CA: Academic Press, 1999.

McAnalley, Bill H. "Chemistry of Alcoholic Beverages." Chapter 1 in *Medicolegal Aspects of Alcohol,* 3rd ed., edited by James C. Garriott. Tucson, AZ: Lawyers and Judges Publishing Company, Inc., 1996.

Mechoulam, R., and Y. Gaoni. "A Total Synthesis of DL-delta-1-Tetrahydrocannabinol, the Active Constituent of Hashish." *J. Am. Chem. Soc.* 87 (1965): 3273–3275.

Miller, Richard Lawrence. *The Encyclopedia of Addictive Drugs.* Westport, CT: Greenwood Press, 2002.

Milles, Dietrich. "History of Toxicology." Chapter 1 in *Toxicology,* edited by Hans Marquardt, Siegfried G. Schäfer, Roger O. McClellan, and Frank Welsch. San Diego, CA: Academic Press, 1999.

National Center for Biotechnology Information. "One Size Does Not Fit All: The Promise of Pharmacogenomics." National Institutes of Health. http://www.ncbi.nlm.nih.gov/About/primer/pharm.html.

National Clearinghouse for Alcohol and Drug Information. "Ketamine. A Fact Sheet." U.S. Department of Health & Human Services. http://ncadi.samhsa.gov/nongovpubs/ketamine/.

Neinstein, Lawrence S., ed. *Adolescent Health Care: A Practical Guide,* 4th ed. Philadelphia: Lippincott Williams & Wilkins, 2002.

NIDA. "Commonly Abused Drugs." National Institute on Drug Abuse. http://www.drugabuse.gov/DrugPages/DrugsofAbuse.html.

NIDA. "Facts on Drugs." National Institute on Drug Abuse. http://teens.drugabuse.gov/facts.

NIDA. "Inhalants." National Institute on Drug Abuse. http://www.nida.nih.gov/ResearchReports/inhalants/inhalants2.html.

NIDA. "NIDA Infofacts." National Institute on Drug Abuse. http://www.nida.nih.gov/infofacts.

Office of Applied Studies. "Drug Abuse Warning Network, 2003: Interim National Estimates of Drug-Related Emergency Department Visits." U.S. Department of Health & Human Services, SAMHSA's National Clearinghouse for Alcohol and Drug Information. http://www.oas.samhsa.gov/dawn/2K3interimED.pdf.

Office of National Drug Control Policy. "Juveniles and Drugs." http://www.whitehousedrugpolicy.gov/drugfact/juveniles/index.html.

"Oregon to Require Prescriptions for Medications Linked to Meth." *New York Times*, August, 17, 2005, A15.

Passie, Torsten, Juergen Seifert, Udo Schneider, and Hinderk M. Emrich. "The Pharmacology of Psilocybin." *Addiction Biology* 7 (2002): 357–364.

Ramchandani, Dilip. "The Librium Story." http://www.benzo.org.uk/librium.htm.

Roueché, Berton. *The Medical Detectives*. New York: Truman Talley Books/Plume, 1991.

Saferstein, Richard. *Criminalistics: An Introduction to Forensic Science,* 8th ed. Upper Saddle River, NJ: Pearson Education, Inc., 2004.

Bibliography

Sandler, David. "Expert and Opinion Testimony of Law Enforcement Officers Regarding Identification of Drug-Impaired Drivers." Chapter 16 in *Medical-Legal Aspects of Drugs,* edited by Marcelline Burns. Tucson, AZ: Lawyers and Judges Publishing Company, Inc., 2003.

Schedules of Controlled Substances. U.S. Code. Title 21, Section 812.

Service, Robert F. "Going from Genome to Pill." *Science* 308 (2005): 1858–1860.

Shulgin, Alexander, and Ann Shulgin. *PiHKAL: A Chemical Love Story.* Berkeley, CA: Transform Press, 1995.

Substance Abuse and Mental Health Data Archive. "Overall Teen Drug Use Continues Gradual Decline; But Use of Inhalants Rises." University of Michigan. http://www.monitoringthefuture.org.

U.S. Drug Enforcement Administration. "Ketamine." http://www.usdoj.gov/dea/concern/ketamine_factsheet.html.

U.S. National Archives and Records Administration. *Code of Federal Regulations,* Title 49, Sec. 40.87 (2005).

U.S. National Library of Medicine. "Drug Information: Barbiturates, Aspirin, and Codeine (Systemic)." Micromedex, Inc. http://www.nlm.nih.gov/medlineplus/print/druginfo/uspdi/202104.htm.

Wilson, R.I., and R.A. Nicoll. "Endocannabinoid Signaling in the Brain." *Science* 296 (2002): 678–682.

Zedeck, Morris S. "A Review and Analysis of the Use of the 2100:1 Blood-Breath Ratio for Determination of Blood Alcohol Concentration: Scientific and Legal Issues." *Expert and Scientific Evidence* 3 (1996): 269–294.

Zedeck, Morris S. "Cocaine Sentencing and Bad Chemistry." *Judicature* 84 (2000): 86–89.

Zernike, Kate. "Officials Across U.S. Describe Drug Woes." *New York Times,* July 6, 2005, A12.

Zernike, Kate. "A Drug Scourge Creates Its Own Form of Orphan." *New York Times,* July 11, 2005, A1.

FURTHER READING

Evans, Colin. *The Casebook of Forensic Detection: How Science Solved 100 of the World's Most Baffling Crimes*. New York: John Wiley & Sons, Inc., 1996.

Fisher, David. *Hard Evidence*. New York: Simon & Schuster, 1995.

Owen, David. *Police Lab*. Buffalo, NY: Firefly Books (U.S.) Inc., 2002.

Wecht, Cyril H. *Crime Scene Investigation*. Pleasantville, NY: The Readers Digest Association, Inc., 2004.

Wecht, Cyril, Greg Saitz, and Mark Curriden. *Mortal Evidence: The Forensics Behind Nine Shocking Cases*. Amherst, NY: Prometheus Books, 2003.

Web Sites

Alcoholics Anonymous
www.aa.org

American Academy of Forensic Sciences (Forensic Science Career Information)
www.aafs.org

Drug Enforcement Administration: Club Drugs
www.usdoj.gov/dea/pubs/intel/01026/index.html

General Information and Photographs of Drugs
www.clubdrugs.org
www.drugabuse.gov/drugpages.html
www.drunkdrivingdefense.com/general/illegal-drugs.htm
www.emedicinehealth.com
www.erowid.org/chemicals
www.streetdrugs.org

Narcotics Anonymous
www.wsoinc.com

National Clearinghouse for Alcohol and Drug Information
www.health.org

National Institute on Drug Abuse (NIDA)
www.nida.nih.gov

Further Reading

Substance Abuse and Mental Health Services Administration
www.samhsa.gov

Information for Teens
http://teens.drugabuse.gov
www.drugabuse.gov/infofax/infofaxindex.html
www.monitoringthefuture.org

Toxicology Tutor
www.sis.nlm.nih.gov/ToxTutor/Tox2/a21.htm

White House Office of National Drug Control Policy
www.whitehousedrugpolicy.gov

PICTURE CREDITS

INDEX

Index

kidneys, 17–18
kinetics. *See* pharmacokinetics

Laborit, Henri, 67
lipids, 13–14, 15, 50–51, 72–73
liver, 15, 17–18, 50, 68–69, 111
LSD, 21, 88, 90–91, 95
lungs, 17–18
Luster, Andrew, 6

Ma Huang, 58–59
MAOI, 22
Marijuana Tax Act, 48
MDMA, 73, 88, 89–90, 92–93, 94
medical examiners, 7
medicinal usage
    of amphetamine, 57–58, 64
    of cocaine, 55, 56
    Controlled Substances Act (CSA) and, 40
    marijuana and, 47, 49
    of opioids, 82
membranes, 12–13, 50–51
mescaline, 89, 92
metabolism
    of alcohol, 68–69
    of barbiturates, 69–71
    of benzodiazepines, 71–73
    of cannabinoids, 50–51
    of GHB, 73–75
    of hallucinogens, 90–95
    of inhalants, 105–106
    of opioids, 83–85
    of PCP and ketamine, 99–100
    of steroids, 110–111
    of stimulants, 60–62
    of THC, 50–51
    tolerance and, 38
    xenobiotic, 15–17
metabolites, activity of, 15–16
methadone, 85
methamphetamine, 58, 61, 65
methaqualone, 75
methcathinone, 58, 62
Mickey Finn, 75
mind-control, 88
monitoring, 44–45
Monitoring the Future (MTF), 41, 44
morphine, 80, 82, 83
motor vehicles, 76–78
mushrooms, 89, 91–92

naloxone, 85
Narcan, 85

narcolepsy, 57, 58
narcotics, defined, 80
National Institute of Justice, 45
nausea, 50
needles, 39
Netter, Frank H., 19
neurotransmitters, 20–23, 74, 88, 100
NHTSA, 76–77
NIDA, 36–37, 44, 109–110
Niemann, Albert, 55
nitrous oxide, 103, 106
NMDA receptors, 22, 84, 100
norepinephrine receptors, 21, 22
noscapine, 80
NSDUH, 43, 44–45
nucleus accumbens, 23
nystagmus, 35, 76

Office of National Drug Control Policy, 45
omega fatty acids, 52
one-leg stand, 76
opioid receptors, 21–22
opioids, 80–87
opium, 80–82
overdoses, 1–2, 71, 75, 76, 85
oxazepam, 73
oxycodone, 43

papaverine, 80
PCP, 22, 97, 99–100, 101
Pemberton, John Styth, 56
phenobarbital, 66
peyote, 89
pH, diffusion and, 13
pharmacodynamic tolerance, 38
pharmacodynamics, 5, 18–23
pharmacogenomics, 17
pharmacokinetic tolerance, 38
pharmacokinetics
    chemical distribution and, 14–15
    defined, 5
    excretion and, 17–18
    future research and, 115
    metabolism and, 15–17
    overview of, 12–14
pharmacology
    animals vs. humans and, 101
    defined, 2, 3–4
    future of forensic, 114–117
    history of, 8
    role of, 7
    toxicology vs., 5
phenanthrenes, 80

ABOUT THE AUTHORS

Beth E. Zedeck grew up in Long Island, New York, and received her BA degree in psychology and her MSW degree in social work with a specialization in alcohol and substance abuse from the State University of New York at Stony Brook. As a licensed certified social worker, Beth spent 15 years in San Francisco and New York City working with adolescents and their families in both psychiatric and substance abuse treatment settings. As her interests grew, Beth attended Columbia University in New York City, from which she received her BS and MS in nursing, and is a certified pediatric nurse practitioner. Beth is a member of several professional organizations and is currently working with children in a medical setting.

Dr. Morris S. Zedeck received his BS degree in pharmacy from the Brooklyn College of Pharmacy, Long Island University; his Ph.D. degree in pharmacology from the University of Michigan; and his MBA degree from the Bernard M. Baruch College, The City University of New York. He completed a postdoctoral fellowship and was assistant professor in the Department of Pharmacology, Yale University School of Medicine. Dr. Zedeck joined the Memorial Sloan-Kettering Cancer Center with a joint appointment at the Cornell University Graduate School of Medical Sciences. He was adjunct associate professor in the Department of Sciences at the John Jay College of Criminal Justice. Dr. Zedeck has published research articles, book chapters, and review articles; edited a book; and is a member of several professional societies. He was president of the Zedeck Advisory Group, Inc., New York, and served as consultant to attorneys and as an expert witness in pharmacology and toxicology. Dr. Zedeck has testified in more than 170 criminal and civil trials involving murder, rape, effects of alcohol and other drugs on driving, testing of controlled substances, medical malpractice, personal injury, and toxic torts.

ABOUT THE EDITOR

Lawrence Kobilinsky, Ph.D., is a professor of biology and immunology at the City University of New York John Jay College of Criminal Justice. He currently serves as science advisor to the college's president and is also a member of the doctoral faculties of biochemistry and criminal justice of the CUNY Graduate Center. He is an advisor to forensic laboratories around the world and serves as a consultant to attorneys on major crime issues related to DNA analysis and crime scene investigation.